Beauty, Truth, Life, and Love

Four Essentials for the Abundant Life

J. BRENT BILL

PARACLETE PRESS

BREWSTER, MASSACHUSETTS

2019 First Printing

Beauty, Truth, Life, and Love: Four Essentials for the Abundant Life

Copyright © 2019 by J. Brent Bill

ISBN 978-1-64060-202-1

Library of Congress Cataloging-in-Publication Data
Names: Bill, J. Brent, 1951- author.
Title: Beauty, Truth, Life, and Love : four essentials for the abundant life / J. Brent Bill.
Description: Brewster, MA : Paraclete Press, Inc., 2019. | Includes bibliographical references.
Identifiers: LCCN 2019019057 | ISBN 9781640602021 (tradepaper)
Subjects: LCSH: Christian life.
Classification: LCC BV4501.3 .B4945 2019 | DDC 248.4—dc23
LC record available at https://lccn.loc.gov/2019019057

10 9 8 7 6 5 4 3 2 1

Published by Paraclete Press
Brewster, Massachusetts
www.paracletepress.com
Printed in the United States of America

CONTENTS

AUTHOR'S NOTE

Throughout the book you'll find little interludes titled "Beauty Rest," "Testing for True," "Life Lines," and "Love Letters." These are meant as short timeouts for reflection on what you have just read. They are based on the Quaker tradition of asking spiritual questions that help us personalize how the Spirit is speaking to us through the text and our daily lives. They are meant to help you examine your life and soul and seek clarity as you search for beauty, truth, life, and love while you move through life. There are no "right" answers—just right for you. They are meant as a pause to give you time to look deeply inside and tap into divine insight.

Please take the time to use them in peacefully listening to God's voice and your own soul in silence. As you contemplate them, allow your mind and soul to fill with words, ideas, or images of beauty, truth, life, and love. If you do, God will gently lead you deeper into the Holy.

CHAPTER 1

The Ideals Life, or The Abundant Life?

I came so that they might have life
and have it more abundantly.

—JESUS

Are you living the abundant life?

An abundant life—not an abundance life. There's a significant difference between the two. Many of us middle-class North Americans are living the abundance life. We have more things than ever. Bigger televisions that grow smarter every day. Technology-laden cars telling us when we've drifted out of our lane or applying our brakes when someone in front of us stops suddenly. Computers more powerful than the ones that helped land men on the moon are held in the palms of our hands Yet, for all our stuff, Henry David Thoreau's nineteenth-century dictum that "the mass of men [and women] lead lives of quiet desperation" is still true.

Despite thousands of books about the good life and countless commercials for products guaranteeing it, Americans are not very happy. A recent survey revealed that the United States was out-happied by Costa Rica—even though our per-capita income is over $47,000 and Costa Ricans earn an average of under $7,000 annually! For all our emphasis on the accoutrements of the good life and our financial ability to obtain them, we Americans don't even make the top-ten happy list. We come in at number fourteen. The good news is we beat out Malta.

Perhaps our lack of happiness or sense that our lives are less than they could be is because our abundance life is rooted in transient things. A dip in the economy can wipe out a lifetime of savings. Trade wars can raise the cost of goods to unaffordable levels, result in the elimination of jobs, put farmers out of business, and more. Plus, all these televisions, tablets, phones, cars, and clothes are constantly being replaced by new and better ones. Advertising, social media, and the like tell us we must have them. And, judging by our buying habits, we believe it.

My main car (I also have a farm pickup and an antique MG that's been in our family since it was new) is just over three years old. It has fewer than thirty-five thousand miles on it. It had everything I wanted on it when I bought it. The good people at Nissan, however, keep sending me information about the newest model—and all the improvements it has over my formerly state-of-the-art automobile. I appreciate their looking out for my automobile welfare, but my car is perfectly fine as it is.

The sad thing is, I'm tempted by all the new gadgets. I want those cool improvements.

They won't, though, bring me the abundant life. When I am silent and still, I realize that the abundant life is a spiritual state of being. The abundance life is an acquisitional way of living.

The abundant life that Jesus came to give us reveals itself in things such as "love, joy, peace, forbearance, kindness, goodness, faithfulness, gentleness and self-control." A new Nissan, even if it does come with "Intelligent Mobility," will not give me any of those things. What will bring them is growing into the person God created me to be, doing the work God meant me to do, being in the relationships I am supposed to have, and so on. I believe that the abundant life is found in four essential ideals. They can guide us into the life Jesus promised if we incorporate them into our daily lives. Those four ideals are beauty, truth, life, and love.

I think one reason that we who desire the abundant life miss living it is that we don't often think about those four things as relating to life of the spirit and faith. I know I don't—or at least I didn't. As you'll see, this is changing for me. Instead we too often consider other things when we think about our work, Christian mission, families, vocations, and relationships. Things such as

- Obligation
- Duty
- Right
- Ought
- Shouldn't

And so we ask questions such as

- What should I do?
- What duty do I as a person of faith have?
- What's the best thing?
- What's the biblical thing?
- What would Jesus do?

The above ideals and questions are not bad. They each have their place in our lives. But they are not the best way to live an abundant life. They leave out the things that bring joy and authenticity to our lives in the Spirit. If we want our spiritual lives to be abundant and full, which is what Scripture tells us they are meant to be, then we need to look for ideals that are deeper and more soul-fulfilling than those of duty, obligation, and Christian correctness.

Beauty, truth, life, and love move us beyond doing life and faith correctly into doing them well. Beauty, truth, life, and love are central to the very essence of the life God desires for us to live. That's because they are the very essence of God. Yet we often neglect beauty, truth, life, and love as we think about our walk with God. We rarely look for them when we consider what God wants for us.

I first began thinking about how beauty, truth, life, and love are essential to faithful living when I was asked to give an address to a gathering of Quakers in Ohio in 2012. Their theme was "Finding Our Way: The Process of Discernment." Some of the Friends (as Quakers are called) on the planning committee had read my book *Sacred Compass: The Way of Spiritual Discernment*. In that book, I proposed that a compass makes a good metaphor for our spiritual lives and the work of discerning God's will. That's because the life of faith can't be programmed into a GPS. It's a meandering pilgrimage along which we may find ourselves wandering. And wondering. Keeping our soul's eyes on our spiritual compass leads us to the holy discovery that we can move through life abundantly. The abundant life we are invited into is one of continuous experiences of God and of spiritual transformation.

The Friends liked what I wrote but wondered if I had learned anything more about discernment since writing that book. If so, would I be willing to share what I'd learned? As I pondered their request I thought about what life and the Spirit had taught me over the last decade. I practiced the things I wrote in *Sacred Compass*, but even so, sometimes I still seemed to have missed the discernment boat. Some things had gone—if not wrong—not exactly right.

I spent time examining those times and things. As I looked closely at them, I realized that in each case at least one of four things was missing. These things were beauty, truth, life, and love. In the things that went right, all four were present, albeit in varying degrees. The more of each of the four was present, the better things went vocationally, relationally, and so on. It became obvious to me that beauty, truth, life, and love must be present in some measure in every important facet of my life. If they're not present, then it's a clear indication that the task, the relationship, the opportunity is not for me. The task is not mine to do. The relationship will not be healthy. The opportunity, no matter how worthy or attractive, is not for me.

So I said yes to the planning committee and began writing my address. I felt energized by it. Indeed, I felt that beauty, truth, life, and love were all present as my thoughts came together.

Then, just before it was time to give my presentation, I was given the chance to put my thesis to work. To move it from theory to practice. That's because I found myself leaving a position that I'd held for more than eleven years. That job was extremely well paying, gave me opportunities to travel and work with fascinating people, had a certain amount of prestige, and more. Suddenly it was time to discern what work I was supposed to do next.

As I began seeking, various job offers and suggestions came my way. All the things that came my way, not surprisingly, were positions similar to the one I had just left. I went for some interviews. The job I left, as you'll learn more about later, had ceased to be life-giving for me and for the organization so long as I was the person holding it. These offers left me cold. I knew I could do them and do them reasonably well. However, they did not make my heart sing.

I prayed. I pondered. Still, as a person quickly approaching retirement, I questioned whether I would dare turn down any position that paid well in exchange for one that fulfilled my new deeper discernment criteria.

Would I really look for beauty, truth, life, and love in what came next?

Or play it safe?

Well, it seemed more than a bit disingenuous at best to stand in front of a group of Quakers and offer them a way into deeper living and not practice that way myself. So, while I continued looking at vocational opportunities, I also began asking if any of those prospective positions fit my new discernment criteria.

None did. And though I can be a non-anxious presence in any number of situations, I was not when it came to the job search. I was hyper-anxious. That's partly because I'm a problem solver. A fixer. I had a problem, and I wanted to throw all my efforts into fixing it—by finding a job.

Through it all, I kept hearing the words of the old hymn "Jesus Calls Us, O'er the Tumult." I was certainly in the tumult. The words that continued to come to mind were these:

Jesus calls us from the worship
of the vain world's golden store,
from each idol that would keep us,
saying, "Christian, love me more."

Honestly, I'm not certain I could love Jesus more than the "vain world's golden store." The latter, however, hadn't served me so well in living the abundant life, so I decided to trust, to relax a bit, and to follow my search for beauty, truth, life, and love in whatever was to come next.

Shortly after I began waiting and trusting, I received an e-mail from a friend about a position that met all those requirements. I tested each one.

- Was there beauty in it?
- Was it true to who I was?
- Would it be life-giving?
- Did my interest in it come from love?

They were all present. So I applied for the position.

Later that month, at the gathering of Friends where I was to speak and while tweaking the manuscript of my address, I received an e-mail inviting me for an interview for the position. And the adventure began. You'll hear more about that later too.

This was the beginning of living a truly experimental life of being guided by beauty, truth, life, and love. I soon found that they were guiding me aright both personally and on my pilgrimage to the face of our loving God. I discovered that when they were each present in some measure in my relationships, ministries, vocations, and life choices, then I was more likely to find myself living more abundantly. They fed my soul with the nourishment necessary for me to grow more fully into the person I was created to be.

I don't claim to have arrived at the perfectly abundant life. I am human and continue to make mistakes . . . or downright failures. Yet, in many ways, I have a deeper sense of life satisfaction, contentment, and happiness since I've sought to live a life of beauty, truth, life, and love.

I believe you will too.

CHAPTER 2
Beauty—Engaging the Divine Spark

———

Begin with the beautiful, and it leads you to the true.
—FATHER ROBERT BARRON

Beauty: the quality or aggregate of qualities in a person or thing that gives pleasure to the senses or pleasurably exalts the mind or spirit.
—Merriam-Webster Dictionary

I surprised myself by going to the opera one night. It was a first for me as someone who has always mocked, albeit gently, opera as little more than a country-western song that lasts three hours and is sung in a foreign language. *Tosca* fit those criteria—it was long (two hours and forty-nine minutes instead of two minutes and forty-nine seconds like many country-western songs) and incredibly sad. All the leads die. "There's blood everywhere," said the docent gleefully prior to the show. Of course, where it differed was that there was no truck or dog or D-I-V-O-R-C-E. Just death and sadness.

What I didn't expect, though, was to be so completely drawn in and mesmerized by *Tosca*. It was beautiful—the sets, the symphony, the singers, the music. Captivating. The time flew by. It was amazing. While I didn't run out and buy season tickets, you can be sure that I'll be putting opera on my list of things to do. It was too beautiful an experience not to enjoy again.

T. C. Henley wrote in an essay, "Beauty is a nectar which intoxicates the soul." *Tosca* certainly intoxicated my soul—just as beauty moves me in soaring works like opera, Manet's impressionism, the architecture of the National Cathedral, an Ansel Adams photograph, a finely turned phrase in a novel, and in the everyday experiences of my life.

So why, if I want to live a God-intoxicated life, do I so often forget that beauty is part of my discernment of what God wants me to do with my life? Why is it I rarely ask, What beauty will come to me by doing this? or, What beautiful thing will result from my doing that?

Why Not Beauty? Reason 1

There are a couple of reasons why we forget that beauty is essential to the life of faith. One is that beauty has such a small place in society today—or at least the idea of beauty. We are becoming a society of technocrats and worker bees focused on outcomes. Production. Busyness.

Production is not wrong, in and of itself. I've produced a good bit of writing in my life. And that's been good for me—including good for my soul.

Busyness, though, seems to not allow room for living.

Even education, as arts programs are cut or removed from curriculum offerings, seems more focused on training rather than broadening human experience, including an introduction to beauty.

I admit I often didn't appreciate every aspect of Music 170—"Music Appreciation"—my first semester at Malone College. My grade in the course attests to that. However, "Music Appreciation" did introduce me to forms of music that I hadn't previously appreciated. I was more interested at that time in people appreciating my guitar playing in a band and listening to rock and roll than Ravel. The only reason my grade was a passing one was because I got extra credit for ushering at performances of the Canton, Ohio, symphony orchestra.

I found live orchestra music fascinating and much more engaging than the scratched-up LPs I listened to on so-so turntables over inadequate headphones in the college library. As bad as my final grade was, my marks went up after listening to live symphonic music. I now have a wide range of classical, baroque, and modern symphonic recordings and attend concerts when I can. The first preset radio button in my car is set to the local classical station.

Our society urges more toward entertainment than engagement with beauty. While beauty can be entertaining, as *Tosca* was, it is much more than entertainment. Entertainment occupies our time; beauty fills it with meaning. Beauty contains truth. One of my favorite lines in Ian McEwan's screenplay of *The Children Act* is "What is beauty in a poem? It's more than just lovely sounds, and it has to be saying something that's true."

Entertainment can be engaging and mind- and soul-numbing at the same time if it does not have beauty. If it is not true.

This is not to disparage entertainment. Sometimes it's just what we need. Like the night I was driving home through a winding, hilly road surrounded by deep woods on both sides. As I came around a curve, a huge deer jumped out of the forest and directly into the path of my car. There was no time for me to stop or for the deer to run and so, even though I hit the brakes, I ran into it going about sixty miles per hour. The impact was terrific, throwing the deer up my hood, hoofs skittering across the windshield, over the roof of the car, and back onto the road. I was momentarily deafened by the noise of the collision. I got out and went to look at the deer. It was dead. I walked back to my car to check it out. The roof was scratched and slightly caved in. The hood was a crumpled mess. The entire front end was caved in, with one headlight out and the other pointing in an odd direction. I was shaking like the leaves in the woods around me.

A fellow stopped. "Can I have the deer?" he asked. "Yep," I said. I knew I didn't want it. The county sheriff came by. "It looks drivable," he said of the car. "Gonna head home?" Home was fifty miles northwest of where I was, but since the closest town had no rent-a-car place or hotel, I decided to make the trek. Two hours later—driving by one working fog light, a headlight that wobbled and pointed in all directions whenever I hit a slight irregularity in the road, and my hazard lights flashing—I pulled into my driveway. "Where have you been?" asked Nancy in that pre-cell-phone age. Then she saw the car and me quaking, though not the Quaker type of quaking. "I'll pour you a glass of wine," she said. My son Chris came out and looked at the car. "I know just what you need," he said. And he led me into the family room to watch a show I'd always scoffed at as stupid. *South Park*. It was stupid. But it was perfect. Just what I needed. I laughed. I enjoyed time with Chris. I stopped obsessing about the deer. At least for a little while.

So, I'm not disparaging entertainment. It has its place in our lives. A prominent place. But not at the price of excluding beauty.

Beauty Rest

Relax your body, mind, and spirit.

Take two or three deep breaths.

Put the book down and think about the following slowly and gently.

Which is larger in my daily life—entertainment or beauty? Why is that?

Entertainment can have beauty certainly. I can be entertained by things that are beautiful, such as a well-made film, or a walk through the National Gallery in Washington, DC, or a stroll through the redwoods at Armstrong Redwoods State Reserve in Guerneville, California. Entertaining experiences are enriched by the presence of beauty.

That's because beauty takes us deeper and provides connection to the best parts of universal human experience. Beauty can break open our hearts and spirits and give us new insights. Think of how seeing a wedding ceremony between two people who you love can bring you to tears—the beauty of their love for each other and the rightness of their coming together in the mystical union of marriage. Think of your own mental catalog of moments or experiences that stunned you with their loveliness. A baby's smile. Lifelong lovers holding hands. A caregiver tenderly tending to a dying loved one. Such naturally beautiful experiences remind our spirits of the amazing gift of simply being alive in this world of wonder and human connection. These are things that defy commodification and cannot be priced, yet are priceless.

While each of these above may not be outside of our everyday existence, that does not make them any less miraculous or beautiful. We can see that they are blessings beyond belief if we truly stop to consider them. What is that mysterious thing that brings two people, previously strangers to each other, together in the beautiful bond of love? How is it that a human egg and tiny sperm connect and transmit life, and blue eyes, and brown hair, and any other of the amazing genetic transfers to that smiling baby? What is it that moves a caregiver to be so compassionate as a part of her or his profession?

In my own life I think of the miracle of the tiny wildflower seeds I sow on top of a winter's snow in January. It doesn't, at first, seem to be the ideal season to spread seed and expect the optimum outcome. Not in the bleak midwinter. And yet, the seeds use the cycles of snow, melt, rain, freeze, snow, and thaw to make their way down to just the right depth to germinate in the spring. They then burst forth in a riot of color and send scintillating scents that bring bees, butterflies, and birds. Each of which adds its own beauty to the prairie.

Likewise, beautiful music or art or writing connects us to the best of human creativity. For example, the play of light in seventeenth-century Dutch artist Jacob van Walscapelle's *Still Life with Fruit* on display at the National Gallery in Washington, DC, amazes me. When I gaze upon it, I am drawn into it. It connects me across centuries with all the others who have viewed this painting and the man who, four hundred years ago, arranged the simple stuff of everyday life and turned it into a lasting, moving piece of beauty. Likewise, when my congregation sings "This Is My Song," my soul enlarges and embraces people around the world when I hear Jean Sibelius's soaring strains and sing Lloyd Stone's wonderful words.

My country's skies are bluer than the ocean
And sunlight beams on clover leaf and pine
But other lands have sunlight, too, and clover
And skies are everywhere as blue as mine
O hear my song, thou God of all the nations
A song of peace for their land and for mine

We people of faith need to help our postmodern, entertainment-based society reclaim a sense of beauty. For the world's sake—and our own.

Beauty Rest _____

Relax your body, mind, and spirit.

Take two or three deep breaths.

Put the book down and think about the following slowly and gently.

What do I experience regularly that combines beauty and entertainment in ways that feed my soul?

Why Not Beauty? Reason 2

I believe the second reason we forget that beauty is essential to the life of faith is because we don't really think of God's will for us—and our discernment of the divine will—as being rooted in beauty. I know that for many years I didn't. Too often God's will seemed like it would be a burden—a going against anything I really desired or I thought would make me happy. It felt like it would have more to do with me giving in than receiving anything positive, let alone beautiful. Of course, that was influenced by the concept I had of God. In many of the stories I'd learned in Sunday school, doing God's will didn't always sound like such a beautiful thing. Look at what happened to poor Job! The prophets were often vilified and hunted down. Stephen got stoned. Christians throughout the ages were martyred.

Perpetua shouted out with joy as the sword pierced her, for she wanted to taste some of the pain and she even guided the hesitant hand of the trainee gladiator towards her own throat.

I'll take a pass, thanks, was my most common reaction. Suffering, persecution, martyrdom was not the kind of beauty I wanted to experience. Oh, me of little faith. It seemed that the wisest course was to do just enough of God's will that wouldn't get me killed. How could dying be beautiful? I admit my view of beauty was limited. I understand now that being willing to die for that which matters most is committing an act of beauty.

Yet, even though I felt the way I just described, there was still something in the deepest part of me that made me want to walk close to God. To be known, as David was despite all his flaws, as a man after God's heart. Which meant daring to do God's will. I recognized beauty in the lives of people I knew who were living God's will. And surviving! One was Leonard Wines. Leonard was the first pastor I remember from my childhood. He came to our church after serving as a missionary in Kenya during extremely dangerous, turbulent times. He went there, along with his young family, because he was following God's beautiful will. As a youngster, I came to know him as a good, kind, and wise man who could be relied on. He had a sense of inner peace and joy that shone in his face and were displayed in his pastoral actions. He also had a sense of fun. What a beautiful soul.

The people I knew like Leonard were changed for the better by doing God's will—even when it was difficult. Doing God's will somehow made them more beautiful, more winsome, more joyous than I knew I was. As I grew, I found their lives were an invitation to reconsider the role of the beautiful in my own spiritual discernment.

That was a wonderful invitation. Also, as I grew, I learned to read the Bible afresh, dropping my old Sunday school lenses from my eyes, and experiencing it in new and deeper ways. That's how I came to read in Ecclesiastes, "He has made everything beautiful in its time."

Certainly, God's will for us is included in that "everything."

Beauty Rest _____

Relax your body, mind, and spirit.

Take two or three deep breaths.

Put the book down and think about the following slowly and gently.

Have I experienced God making "everything beautiful in its time"?
If so, how did I recognize that? If not, what might open my spiritual eyes
to that divine reality?

As I thought about my "old Sunday school lenses," I also thought about how the church I grew up in was none too concerned with beauty. We were focused on learning the Bible and teaching people the way to salvation. We had an organ and choir, which was usual for the pastoral branch of Quakers that I belonged to. But we didn't have much else in the way of the arts, other than Warner Sallman's *Head of Christ* or *Christ at Heart's Door* paintings in some Sunday school rooms.

One reason for that is that from our beginning Quakers were a plain people. The early Friends dressed simply, mostly in blacks, browns, and grays. Their homes and meetinghouses were plain, without ornamentation. Engagement in the arts was discouraged as frivolous and taking time away from spiritual study and prayer. Quakers who wanted to be musicians, artists, fiction writers, poets, and more risked being disowned (excommunicated) from their meeting (church). Nineteenth-century Quaker minister and artist Edward Hicks, who is now famous as an early American folk artist, primarily for his paintings of the peaceable kingdom from Isaiah 6, faced severe opposition from his fellow Friends for his pursuit of his art.

This anti-art attitude has lasted a long while among some Friends. I remember as a young adult visiting one group of Quakers who held to the traditional ways of speaking, dressing, and feelings toward the arts. One of their young men had gone to college and studied music. He developed into an amazingly gifted classical pianist. He returned home and asked if he could share his gift of music with Friends in the meetinghouse. This request was met with much deliberation and concern by these Friends. Finally, after more than an hour of intense sharing, the decision was made that he could not. He could, however, play in the gymnasium of the local Friends school just across the parking lot.

I found their denial of his offering to share his God-given gift as an act of worship heartbreaking. My spirit ached for him, though he did play in the proffered place.

This attitude against the arts is changing among Quakers, for which I'm grateful. However, I don't believe that Friends are the only denomination with this attitude. Too many congregations, especially free church or evangelical ones, are fine with religious music and a smattering of devotional art, but rarely encourage their members toward creativity and beauty. We may offer classes in the Bible—but what about beauty? Scripture, but not song. Prayer, but not play-acting.

And then we wonder why we do not see the will of God as beautiful instead of stern and demanding. This, I think, makes the church complicit in our believing that beauty need not come into play when we discern the divine will. If our churches talked more about beauty—in God's work in the world, in the arts, and in people's lives—then we would be more likely to think that God's will might be something beautiful. Something soul-pleasing. Something spirit-filling. Something life-giving.

As we consider what God wants us to do, we need to seek beauty in the desires God has for us.

Beauty Rest _____

Relax your body, mind, and spirit.

Take two or three deep breaths.

Put the book down and think about the following slowly and gently.

Does my place of worship encourage engagement with beauty? Could there be room for more beauty? What might my role be in helping that to happen?

Living a Beautiful Faith

What would it be like for us to live a beautiful faith? How would our lives change if we lived seeking beauty and then living beautifully in response to the Spirit's leading? One way our lives would change is that we would feel closer to God. God is beautiful. We often think of God in terms of majesty, power, omniscience, omnipresence, transcendence, and the like. But above all, God possess amazing beauty. The psalmist says he seeks "to gaze on the beauty of the LORD."

After going to the opera that night, I am more than ever convinced of the wisdom of such a wild idea as living a beautiful faith. After all, my preconceptions of opera were shattered not by rational arguments by leading critics, not by a pledge of rigid adherence to Puccini's original score or staging, and not because the opera house provided an "opera-seeker-sensitive" listening experience with cupholders at each seat, watered-down content, and a sitcom length. No. Instead, my ideas about opera were changed because the participants cared enough to make it beautiful. And that beauty made me long to experience more.

That's because beauty is life-giving. It reminds us that we are alive. The wonderfully wise writer Frederick Buechner wrote,

> Have you wept at anything during the past year?
>
> Has your heart beat faster at the sight of young beauty?
>
> Have you thought seriously about the fact that someday you are going to die?
>
> More often than not, do you really listen when people are speaking to you, instead of just waiting for your turn to speak?
>
> Is there anybody you know in whose place, if one of you had to suffer great pain, you would volunteer yourself?
>
> If your answer to all or most of these questions is no, the chances are that you're dead.

If we learn to live beautifully, we will be more spiritually satisfied. More alive. And we will also be offering a winsome invitation to others to meet our beautiful God.

This divinely inspired beauty can appear in many ways, including making something beautiful for the world or fulfilling our longing for beauty in our souls.

Beauty Rest

Relax your body, mind, and spirit.

Take two or three deep breaths.

Put the book down and think about the following slowly and gently.

What are ways I could live a beautiful faith?

Finding the Divine in All Beauty

Russian novelist Fyodor Dostoevsky says, "Beauty will save the world." That's a great quotation. It was used as a tagline by *Image*, one of my favorite literary and arts journals. I liked it but first thought, *I flat out don't believe that.* Of course, I might have been influenced by that quote's coming from a book titled *The Idiot*.

The more I thought about it, though, I decided I did believe it. For two reasons. One is that beauty points us to God, which leads to our salvation. Our souls hunger for beauty wherever they can find it. They do so because our hunger for beauty is a hunger for God, whether we're aware of it or not. We yearn in the deepest part of ourselves for a real and profound connection to the divine. That desire for connection is part of our DNA—it is rooted in our bodies *and* souls. We are drawn to beauty as we are drawn to the divine. The poet Martin Farquhar Tupper says, "Our primal source was beauty, and we pant for it ever and again."

The panting Tupper refers to is not just metaphorical. It's not just spiritual. It's physical. Physical experience is something we often forget when we think about matters of faith and the life of the spirit. And yet we were created body *and* soul! Not just soul. And while we spend much of our religious life *thinking* about God and spiritual matters, we often learn most in daily life through physical experiences. Through our senses. That's why poet and potter M. C. Richards says, "It is in our bodies that redemption takes place. . . . I learn through my hands and my eyes and my skin what I could never learn through my brain."

Beauty is one of the ways we learn through our hands, our eyes, our skin, our noses, and our ears. My ears behold beauty regardless of whether I'm listening to Bach's Sonata no. 5 or the Beatles' *Abbey Road* or old tapes of my son Ben's garage band The Banned. My eyes take in beauty while looking at Jackson Pollock's *Convergence* or the copy of Sylvia Shaw Judson's *Bird Girl* sitting in my yard or a painting by my great-granddaughter Evelyn. I taste beauty when I sip a fine Zinfandel or bite into one of Nancy's yeast rolls hot from the oven.

Those, and many more, are how I learn through my hands and my eyes and my skin. Yours will be different. My kids and grandkids and siblings and friends all experience bodily beauty differently. The old saying that "Beauty is in the eye of the beholder" is not just a cliché; it's true.

Beauty Rest ───────────────────

Relax your body, mind, and spirit.

Take two or three deep breaths.

Put the book down and think about the following slowly and gently.

Where is beauty in my daily life? In the things around me?
  Does beauty help save my world?

When I went for walks with my late, greatly loved Great Pyrenees Bonnie through the prairie and woods that make up the majority of Ploughshares Farm, I could just enjoy the pleasant surroundings. Or I could do so with the intention of paying attention to the signs of life around me. When I walk the latter way, I walk more slowly. My breathing is less labored. Stress begins to melt away. I see things I don't see when I'm "just walking." I see raccoon and beaver tracks in the sandy soil where the creek used to run. I see nests in the trees harboring birds and squirrels. I see the subtle signs of deer trails disappearing into the woods and can follow them if so inclined. If I do it carefully, I am sometimes surprised by the beauty of a silent fawn or full-grown deer standing stock still, alert to my presence before bounding away to safety.

In his poem "From a Country Overlooked," Tom Hennen reminds me that all around me are God's creatures inviting me to witness and experience beauty. Such as the two wild turkey hens and their three hatchlings who walked ahead of me in the woods today, as we all headed toward the prairie.

Though I know that's true, it is a beauty near at hand— in the country I often overlook. The space I live in. This prairie and these woods and this house. The country you often overlook is likely far different from mine. It may be the country of suburban homes or a high-rise apartment in the city. It may be in a desert or verdant deep forest or on frozen Alaskan tundra or on a warm sunny beach. Regardless, God is present in beauty all around us. God's imprint is everywhere if only we take time to look with the expectation of seeing it. With our souls open to beauty and grace.

Beauty Rest _____

Relax your body, mind, and spirit.

Take two or three deep breaths.

Put the book down and think about the following slowly and gently.

How do I open my body, mind, and spirit to seeing God's beauty present all around me?

The important thing for me about beauty is that it is not just about appreciating beauty for beauty's sake. No. Rather beauty points us to what is truly beautiful—the face of our loving God. Even when we are not aware of it. God is in all beauty—maybe not to the same extent in each piece of beauty—human-made or natural—we encounter, but certainly there in some measure. And if we look for that divine presence, we can find it. As Jim Croegaert's song "Why Do We Hunger for Beauty?" asks,

Frost on the window never the same
So many patterns fit in the frame
Captured in motion frozen in flame
And in the patterns is there a Name?

"And in the patterns is there a Name?" Indeed, there is. If we are looking for it, that is.

Looking for that name is not hard to do if we remember that we were created for wonder. As children we didn't need to be reminded of that. The whole world was filled with wonder. Everything around us was amazing. The magic of Christmas and surprise of birthday presents. The amazement of blue skies with fluffy, towering clouds forming rabbits and faces and more. The astonishing first taste of cotton candy at the county fair. Wonders all around us to be experienced and enjoyed. Anne Lamott reminds us of that when she says,

Try walking around with a child who's going, "Wow, wow! Look at that dirty dog! Look at that burned-down house! Look at that red sky!" And the child points and you look, and you see, and you start going, "Wow! Look at that huge crazy hedge! Look at that teeny little baby! Look at the scary dark cloud!" I think this is how we are supposed to be in the world—present and in awe.

When is the last time you experienced wonder? A wonder that thrilled you to your very core? A wonder that comes from God and is recognized as such? Children are good at recognizing God. As the poet Hafiz reminds us,

> Every child has known God,
> Not the God of names,
> Not the God of don'ts,
> Not the God who ever does
> Anything weird,
> But the God who knows only 4 words
> And keeps repeating them, saying:
> "Come Dance with Me."
> Come Dance.

So how do we look for God in all beauty? How do we encounter a beauty that makes us fully present, in awe, and seeing the presence of God? We begin by recovering a childlike sense that we are alive in a world of wonder and beauty and God. Not the God of "don'ts" but the God who takes us by the hand and says, "Come dance with Me." The God who created all beauty and says, "Take and eat."

Beauty Rest

Relax your body, mind, and spirit.

Take two or three deep breaths.

Put the book down and think about the following slowly and gently.

What are some things I can do to become more childlike and open to wonder and beauty?

For some of us, finding God in all beauty will mean reconnecting with the natural world, as when I walk in the woods. For others it can be getting up from our desks at lunchtime, walking through the city with a bite to eat, settling on a bench near a tree, and feeling the breeze and sunlight beaming down.

"Let all creation help you to praise God," says Saint Paul of the Cross.

Give yourself the rest you need. When you are walking alone, listen to the sermon preached to you by the flowers, the trees, the shrubs, the sky, the sun and the whole world. Notice how they preach to you a sermon full of love, of praise of God, and how they invite you to proclaim the greatness of the one who has given them being.

That works for me. Whether at home on the farm or walking through a big-city neighborhood, I feel rested, floating on the eternal nature of God's love, enjoying the sounds around me. At such times I find myself falling toward grace, falling into the great Love of God. Richard C. Cabot says, "Whenever beauty overwhelms us, whenever wonder silences our chattering hopes and worries, we are close to worship."
Indeed.

When we seek beauty, or serendipitously experience it, we find ourselves falling *toward*, instead of from, grace. Perhaps that's because the memory of Eden, life with God walking in the cool of the evening, is locked deep within our bones and souls, deeper than any genetic code. There is an eternal ongoing presence of life.

Marianne Borouch writes,

In my old Catholic neighborhood in Chicago, we used to hear about the contemplatives, certain orders of nuns we never saw, cloistered away somewhere. . . . Then we heard about the holy rumble, their job only to pray, words rushed like music, something near chant.

And one of our teachers told us—Sister Norbuertus or Sister Mary Hubertine?—that this sacred hum, exactly this, kept the earth turning on its axis, not merely this day or this minute, but for all worlds of the past and the future because life is linked and there are no divisions in time. It's a plain fact, she told us with nary a blink, like science is fact.

For proof, she instructed us to close our eyes and listen hard. And she was right. We could hear them. The world was linked. That low-grade roar locked in our heads, steady undercurrent of rushing blood and flashing nerve—was it only that? Maybe it was those women after all, pulling from the world its oldest sound, ever dark and light in the universe subdued, backdrop to thought, to words, to laughter, to every sorrow coming up slowly, inevitably a forewarning or a reminder. Certain moments, if I become very still, even now I hear it.

"Certain moments, if I become very still, even now I hear it."

That's something we need to do—become very still. All around us is beauty, given to us by a grace-full God who loves us and comes to us, walking in the cool of the evening. Take time to enjoy the sounds and smell of life-grace around you. Stop, literally, and smell the roses or ethnic food cooking in the co-op next door or vine-ripening tomatoes in the community garden. Listen to the birds and happy conversations. Feel the sun warm on your face or the love of those close to you. Know that God loves you and holds you, even in the days when it doesn't feel like it, deep in the divine heart, and that no permanent harm will be allowed to befall you.

Take time for a daily round (or rounds!) of beauty. Make time for joy, pleasure, delight, charm, sweetness, and loveliness. Take time to fall toward grace. Our longing for beauty in nature, the arts, and other people points us to the One who created it all.

Beauty Rest _____

Relax your body, mind, and spirit.

Take two or three deep breaths.

Put the book down and think about the following slowly and gently.

What would I have to do to carve out some time for a daily round of beauty for myself? Would I best experience beauty in stillness or activity? In nature or at a cinema?

Creating Beauty

The second reason I believe that beauty can save the world is that our hunger for beauty is linked to our desire to create. That desire to create is a mark of our being created in the image of our Creator God.

The first thing we see in Scripture is God's creative nature. "In the beginning God created the heavens and the earth." God brought order and beauty out of chaos. In that same way, a potter takes chaos in the form of clay and shapes it into something beautiful. Or a baker uses ingredients springing from the earth and its bounty and makes a cake. Or a supervisor sees the potential in the disparate talents of a company's workers and helps fashion them into an amazingly inventive team. Or we, as individuals, come to see our lives as creative works and seek to make them obedient in beauty, not just duty.

Too many of us, for whatever "good" reasons, have put away much of our creativity as we've aged. We've put away the Play-Doh, making music with kazoos or guitars, quit telling one another fantastic stories, and the like. We have quit doing many of the things that gave us joy and hope and meaning—and created beauty—when we were young.

The same, sorry to say, is often true about putting away the things of faith that brought us joy and helped us create beauty. Think of the times when you were closest to the divine—feeling the Spirit's spark in a way that was compelling and beautiful.

"Whenever you are creating beauty around you, you are restoring your own soul," says Alice Walker. And even more—you are restoring the world. And thereby beauty is saving the world!

That's because, as Rabbi Abraham Joshua Heschel explains,

creation, we are taught, is not an act that happened once upon a time, once and for ever. The act of bringing the world into existence is a continuous process. God called the world into being, and that call goes on. There is this present moment because God is present. Every instant is an act of creation.

While we often think of creativity in terms of art or music or poetry, it is so much more. Any act that employs our best talents—the ones that feed our minds as well as our souls—is creative. Composing a cantata, putting together a work plan that brings out your staff's talents and fires their imaginations, or filling out the roster for the church softball team in such a way that everybody gets to play is creativity in the image of God. When we invoke our imaginations and our souls are working cooperatively, then we are taking part in one of those instants that is an act of creation Heschel spoke of, because God is present.

Beauty Rest

Relax your body, mind, and spirit.

Take two or three deep breaths.

Put the book down and think about the following slowly and gently.

Have I ever thought of what I do at work as creating beauty?
  How do my daily tasks summon both my spirit and my imagination?

"Let the beauty we love be what we do," wrote Rumi. The beauty we love inspires us to creation. I love crafting books and stories out of the ethereal objects that are words. I also love following deer tracks through the woods and clearing and widening their paths so that others can walk in the way the deer—being creative according to their nature—have.

I know others who work with numbers or science—solving the riddles of the universe. Still others look at things that some would see as problems, but because they love problem-solving, they come up with creative solutions that benefit themselves and others.

My friend Alan Garinger was such a person. When he got tired of lugging the wood chipper I had given him and equally tired of emptying the bag that filled with chips of branches and leaves, he put on his thinking cap. First, he took an old two-wheel hand truck he had in his barn and drilled a hole through its platform and through the skid plate on the wood chipper. Then he fastened a long screw up through the bottom of the hand truck and inserted it into the hole in the skid plate. He tilted the hand truck back, and the chipper moved easily. Next, he removed the collection bag and the piece to which the bag attached. He bought some used furnace ductwork at the local secondhand store. Using tin snips, Alan fashioned a chute that would funnel the chips up and out into the wagon he pulled behind his yard tractor. Both of his inventions were elegant and simple solutions—creativity that both fulfilled a need and made Alan proud and pleased. He was doing the beauty he loved—problem-solving. And it was practical to boot.

Such creativity is beauty in the eye of the beholder. You may have noticed that I haven't described what beauty is. While art critics and others are happy to tell us what beauty is, the truth is that what is beautiful to one is not necessarily beautiful to another. Our hearts, working with our five senses and mind, tell us what is beautiful.

Transforming the Ugly

In the same way that our hearts, working with our five senses and mind, tell us what is beautiful, they also tell what is ugly. Beauty implies a certain "rightness." Ugly doesn't feel right. It is discomfiting. It's jarring and out of place. There is a lot of ugliness in this world. The current state of politics in the United States (and other places) certainly points to that—the ugliness of lies, name-calling, and mean policies that harm people. There's the ugliness of hungry children, wars, and more.

The farmer poet Wendell Berry says, "If a thing is ugly, I think we need to ask questions about it. How did it get that way? What else is wrong?"

When I ask Berry's questions, another question comes to mind—"Can it be transformed?" That resonates with my Christian faith, which is all about transformation and redemption. I think of all the people who were, metaphorically and literally, ugly and misshapen in Scripture and who were touched by Jesus and changed into people of inestimable beauty. Might such transformation be part of our calling when confronted with the ugly?

If we are seeking beauty and creativity, I believe we will find fresh ways of creating beauty even when confronted with the ugly. We will discover ways of transforming it. There's an ugly old farm dump on part of Ploughshares. For you city slickers (of which I was one for about fifty-three years), a farm dump is where old equipment and worn-out appliances and other things go after they die. In the case of the one on Ploughshares, it's in a ravine prone to erosion due to springs of water flowing out of the hillside. Over the years, the people whose farm this was before me dumped old stoves, water heaters, used fencing, a pickup-truck bed, and more into this ravine.

When I first saw it, I saw it as ugly. It seemed like a scar on the land. My son-in-law and I, who often work in the woods and prairie together, talked about ways of clearing it out, including hiring someone to come clean it in exchange for the value of the scrap metal they could make.

But then I thought about the questions Berry asked. I knew how it got that way—it was a convenient place to dump. It was also a way to keep the hillside ravine from eroding. What else was wrong was that there were several things in there that would not be worth a person's time cleaning it out and restoring it.

We cleaned the land at the top of the dump, but then allowed some bushes to grow up and begin reclaiming the area. The junk then anchored the hillside as the roots of bushes and trees began springing up through and around it, arresting the erosion from the springs.

While doing this, I also found the farm dump was a place that possessed its own kind of beauty. I discovered it when I peered through the lens of my Nikon, focusing on the once-sturdy agricultural machinery and old appliances that rust was wearing away. As I looked for beauty in the small bits, they chipped the big, ugly whole away.

I have friends who have found beauty in reclaiming what others have proclaimed ugly. My friend the late Phil Ball made art from found and discarded items. One piece was fashioned from an old bicycle fork, seat, and handlebars along with a small varmint trap. He called it *The*

Tender Trap—you'll have to use your imagination to figure out what he crafted. My buddy Dan has a shed and barn filled with other people's discards. He creates beauty by repairing things that people throw out. Like when the pump on the sprayer I use in caring for my prairie failed, I took it to Dan's. Within an hour he had taken it apart, looked through his assortment of stuff, selected some pieces, used them to replace the parts in my pump, and had it working again.

Dan, like Alan, also invents things out of the stuff he redeems. When he came to help me burn the prairie (prescribed burns are a part of prairie maintenance), he showed up with a gadget constructed out of an old propane tank from a grill, a two-wheel handcart, some propane hose, and a nozzle. He opened the valve on the tank, used a spark to light the gas flowing from the nozzle, and voilà, off we went strolling the edge of the prairie and lighting it on fire with an ease we'd never had before. All because ugly had been made useful and beautiful.

All around the world there are people doing such things and more. Transforming ugliness. Giving their lives to feed hungry children. Working to bring peace in war-torn areas. Eradicating diseases. Putting in wells for clean drinking water.

Beauty Rest _____

Relax your body, mind, and spirit.

Take two or three deep breaths.

Put the book down and think about the following slowly and gently.

Where do I regularly encounter ugliness? Are there things I can do to transform it into something more positive, more beautiful?

I also think that in the same way we see external ugliness, we need to be able to recognize any ugliness within our lives. I often wonder if ugliness is a sort of rebellion—an assertion of my self-will like the petulant spiritual two-year-old I am (no offense to two-year olds!). While I may publicly sing the old gospel song "Have Thine Own Way, Lord," in my heart I'm often singing "Have Mine Own Way, Brent." I realized the truth of how my own selfish willfulness kept me from transforming ugly into beautiful when I read Laurence Boldt's words that

> the truth is, until we have taken the time to discover and affirm who we really are and what we really want, we are left with only negative identities and negative passion. We define ourselves by what we are against, and so have negative, not creative, passion. We need something to rebel against or we don't feel like we exist. We need someone to rebel against or we don't feel passionate about anything. . . . We are comfortable with rebelling, but fearful of creating.

Seen that way, beauty is redemptive. That's because, as the writer Dave Eggers says, "We see the beauty within and cannot say no."

Beauty Rest _____

Relax your body, mind, and spirit.

Take two or three deep breaths.

Put the book down and think about the following slowly and gently.

How is beauty redemptive in my own life?

Creativity—whether in the art studio or lived out as spiritual pilgrims discerning the divine will—invites us to take part in God's redemption of this world and our own lives. God calls us to bring beauty and order from chaos; to bring glad tidings of great joy; and to live, as Gordon Crosby said, with such "a striking resemblance to Jesus that people sense they have encountered him when they encounter us."

Dare we live a beautiful faith and thereby live more abundantly?

Dare we not?

CHAPTER 3
Truth—Living in Utter Rightness

If our true nature is permitted to guide our life,
we grow healthy, fruitful and happy.
—ABRAHAM MASLOW

Truth carries life-giving properties for the soul, and without these
properties the soul languishes and shrinks. Whether it be pleasant
or bitter its effect is healthgiving.
—HAL M. HELMS

One of my favorite photos shows six fellows sitting on the top beam of what looks to be a barn's timber frame. Thirty feet above the ground, their booted, blue-jeaned, Carhartt-jacketed and ball-capped figures are a stark contrast to the blue April sky.

There are a couple of reasons I love that picture. For one, it's a fun one. Six guys sit on a beam thirty feet in the air with their faces shining with satisfaction. They're smiling with their hammers resting in their toolbelt loops. As they look down from their lofty perch, they are completely comfortable with where they're sitting. They've built this frame and pronounced it good and sturdy. A job well done.

Another reason I like it is that it's a photograph of my post-and-beam home's frame and the men who built it. Post-and-beam homes aren't the norm around central Indiana. The one we live in was made from recycled wood from old armament factories. Our house came ready to build, shipped out on four semis from Yankee Barn Homes in New Hampshire. The posts and beams were all cut, notched, and numbered in the order in which the frame was to be assembled.

The framing crew, the men posing on top of that beam, were from just up the road. They'd never built such a home before. They set to it with vigor. They used two-pound sledgehammers to drive eight- and twelve-inch spikes into the posts and beams to secure them. I drove—ceremonially—one or two of the spikes. I was mostly a go-fer—going for more posts and beams and nails and water for the guys doing the work.

Another one of my jobs was to bring twelve-foot-long two-by-fours to them to use as bracing. Every post had to be braced to keep it plumb. Every beam that tied in needed to be held level. Over four days we went from a flat plywood deck to a fully constructed post-and-beam frame that was perfectly true from every angle.

Though my Grandpa Bill had passed away thirty years before we started building this house, every time we checked the trueness, I thought of him and his plumb line. He was a man of few words and reasoned thinking. Everything he did was carefully considered, from building his garage to reading his Bible. When he built things, which he did often, he'd check them with a square, a bubble level, and then he'd often pull out a plumb line. His was made from a long piece of sturdy string tied to a two-pound plumb bob that tapered to a point. He'd unwind the line, hold it up to the frame he was building, and let plumb bob drop. Then he'd look to see if the board lined up perfectly with that string. If it did, he knew it was true. He trusted his eyes, but he trusted the truth of the plumb bob more.

Building our house, we, on the other hand, didn't use a plumb bob. We checked the frame's trueness with long bubble levels and laser levels as we moved through the construction. Each post had to be level on the bubble from every side or line up with the red beam the laser shot out. Likewise with each beam.

When we finished it was level on the level. It was true.

The frame, because it was true, was also beautiful. It had a satisfying symmetry that was pleasing to the eye. The cherry-stained posts and beams, even with their many nicks, gouges, nail holes, and imperfections from having lived in old factories for decades, looked beautiful against the spring sky.

But of course, for all its beauty and trueness, the frame was not livable as it was. To become a hospitable house it needed walls, a roof, windows, doors, and more. Before any of that could be added, though, the frame had to be built true—to be plumb. That way the premade outer wall and roof panels that Yankee Barn shipped to us would fit in place. The windows would open easily and doors swing open and shut correctly.

The early proof that the frame was truly true was when the carpenters began hanging those premade outer walls. The sidewalls were nine feet tall and varied in length from six to twelve feet. They were eight inches thick with layers of framing, foam insulation, house wrap, and installed siding or windows for the exterior and faced with drywall for the interior. To say they were heavy is an understatement. The panels were fitted with lifting plates, and the fellow on the big orange four-wheel-drive forklift hooked them up and then swung them into place. Each one fit, with a minor tap or two.

As the walls were swung into place and attached, I began removing the bracing. The trueness of the construction held. It holds to this day. Windows open easily without binding. Skylights lift and shut securely. Doors open and close, the latch snicking securely into the strike plate. The house is solid, warm, and welcoming to all who visit.

So, what's all this got to do with "truth"? The kind of truth I'm speaking about in this chapter is the kind of true of our house's frame. Plumb true, as some people say. The kind of true that fits with integrity into our lives.

Even the Bible talks about that kind of plumb true. In Isaiah 28, God says,

I will make justice the measuring line
and righteousness the plumb line.

And the prophet Amos says,

> This is what he showed me: The Lord was standing by a wall that
> had been built true to plumb, with a plumb line in his hand. And
> the Lord asked me, "What do you see, Amos?"
> "A plumb line," I replied.
> Then the Lord said, "Look, I am setting a plumb line among my
> people Israel; I will spare them no longer."

Now these passages aren't particularly pleasant to peruse. God uses a plumb line to judge and finds Israel (and by implication, us) wanting. They do, however, illustrate the type of true I'm talking about as we seek the abundant life. The true we look for is found in the true that can be tested and seen. That kind of true has an integrity that holds the whole together in just rightness. And perhaps even in righteousness, à la Isaiah 28.

Testing for True _____

Relax your body, mind, and spirit.

Take two or three deep breaths.

Put the book down and think about the following slowly and gently.

What is an example of something that's plumb true in my life?

Speaking of Truth

While dining out one evening, the server approached our table and asked, "Do you have any questions?" "Yes," I replied, "what is truth?" She shook her head, probably thinking, *Oh no, one of those customers*. My companion shook her head, grimaced, and looked sympathetically at the server. "You'd better tip her well," she said after our order was taken. Indeed.

But the question remains—What is truth? That's one of humankind's oldest questions. It's been the subject of serious discourses, sermons, lectures, friendly ruminations, and silly skits. (Check out Steve Martin's "The Death of Socrates" on YouTube.) The American philosopher Williams James wrote *The Meaning of Truth* in 1914, but his book hardly settled the matter. In 2010, Christopher P. Long reached back to the fourth century BCE when writing *Aristotle on the Nature of Truth*, with chapters such as "Toward a Phenomenology of Truth." I truthfully don't know what phenomenology is (according to Wikipedia it's "the philosophical study of the structures of experience and consciousness") or why I should even care why Aristotle thought it was important. Maybe he didn't, since phenomenology is a twentieth-century construct!

Church fathers (primarily) through the ages, such as Augustine, Thomas Aquinas, and Anselm (and that's just the "A's"!), have added their thoughts. "If there is something more excellent than the truth, then that is God; if not, then truth itself is God," posits Augustine. Anselm defined truth as "a rectitude perceptible by the mind alone." Aquinas seems to agree, and says, "Truth resides, in its primary aspect, in the intellect."

I remember discussing much of this in various college classes. Deep thoughts for those of us who thought we were deep—or pretended to be. I graduated from a small, private Quaker college in southwestern Ohio. Wilmington College, in addition to the usual liberal arts majors, also had (and still does) an agriculture major. One day, in a Kelly

Center classroom, we were discussing Schopenhauer on truth. One of the ag students, fresh in from working at the college's swine barn and a little ripe smelling, exclaimed, "Yeah, well, what's that got to do with real life?"

What indeed. What good are philosophical and religious discourses on truth if they are primarily teleological concepts (such as whether the reason something exists is determined by a set purpose for which it was created) that have no connection to daily life? Daily life—the ordinary stuff—is, obviously, the place that most of us inhabit while striving to live lives that are true.

Testing for True _____

Relax your body, mind, and spirit.

Take two or three deep breaths.

Put the book down and think about the following slowly and gently.

When I think of "true", which comes to mind—philosophical truth or

real-life truth? What's the difference between the two to me?

Now, in our own time, the philosopher and presidential attorney Rudy Giuliani tried to make truth consistent with his client's real life. While being interviewed on *Meet the Press* Giuliani famously said, "Truth isn't truth," while implying that there are different versions of the truth.

"What is truth?" That depends on the kind of truth we're seeking, especially in this time when trueness feels in low quantity. In 2005, Stephen Colbert coined a term that seemed funny at the time—"truthiness." According to Colbert, "Truthiness is 'What I say is right, and [nothing] anyone else says could possibly be true.' It's not only that I *feel* it to be true, but that *I* feel it to be true. There's not only an emotional quality, but there's a selfish quality."

Today "truthiness" is all around us. The deep ponderings about truth by Socrates, Kant, and other philosophers through the ages have been replaced by "*I feel* it to be true."

Does feeling it to be true make it true? Is there any real trueness?

In many houses of faith, the answer is yes. Scriptural truth is held to be the truest truth since it comes from God. That view is rooted firmly in the words of the Bible. The psalmist pleads,

Show me your ways, LORD,
teach me your paths.
Guide me in your truth and teach me,

Jesus says he is the truth. He also said that if we follow his teachings," then you will know the truth, and the truth will set you free."

Philosophical truth.

Theological truth.

Teleological truth.

Political truth.

Biblical truth.

There certainly seem to be a lot of truths.

How is a person who wants to be true to discover the truth? Being true is important for many reasons. Not least among them is revealed in the words of the hymn, "I would be true, for there are those who trust me."

We as people of God need to look at biblical truth, but we also need to look beyond it. We also need to look for truth in the sense of rightness and integrity with our daily lives.

Rarely do people of faith talk about the plumb truth of everyday life. It's not often that we ponder how that kind of truth fits our spiritual experiences. Those who talk about truth often forget that the heart of the truth we're seeking is not found in esoteric notions of truth. The truth we seek to live lies in the daily places where we exist. Our homes. Our work. Our relationships. Our recreation.

Wendell Berry says,

We cannot know the whole truth, which belongs to God alone, but our task nevertheless is to seek to know what is true. And if we offend gravely enough against what we know to be true, as by failing badly enough to deal affectionately and responsibly with our land and our neighbors, truth will retaliate with ugliness, poverty, and disease.

We want to live by what we know—not just "feel" like in "truthiness"—to be true. We want to live that way both to avoid ugliness, poverty, and disease, whether physical or emotional or spiritual, and because deep in our souls we sense that we were made for rightness. Seeking the truth—the rightness that jibes with ordinary experience is the kind of truth that is more than propositional, or that can be reasoned about and figured out in our brains, or is how *I feel*. It is felt, to be sure, deep in our souls, our bodies, and our minds. Felt in our whole being. As early Quaker Margaret Fell wrote,

I saw it was the truth, and I could not deny it; and I did as the apostle saith, I "received the truth in the love of it." And it was opened to me so clear that I had never a tittle in my heart against it; but I desired the Lord that I might be kept in it, and then I desired no greater portion.

Testing for True _____

Relax your body, mind, and spirit.

Take two or three deep breaths.

Put the book down and think about the following slowly and gently.

When have I experienced a truth that I could not deny? Did I receive that truth in love and embrace it?

Margaret Fell's experience of that which is true was that it was true in all its forms. I love how she says, "I saw it was the truth, and I could not deny it." There is something about truth that is undeniable. Even if we wish to deny it. The truth is not dependent on whether we believe something is true. Some things are just true. Gravity is true—whether we believe in gravity or not. If the reality, the truth, of gravity was dependent on our believing in it, then there would be a goodly number of folks who didn't believe in it out soaring around while those of us who did believe would remain with our feet firmly planted on the ground.

We may wish to deny the truth of something because it's inconvenient or doesn't fit with what we want. But that doesn't make it any less true or deniable in the deepest part of our being. Something deep in our being—springing from being created in God's image—recognizes truth, even if we don't resonate with it or if we openly resist it.

Fell embraced it and desired, as she said, to be kept in it.

Likewise, mere belief doesn't make something true. Believing that separating mothers and children making their way across the border is an act of Christian charity doesn't make it so. We know that because it is out of plumb with Amos's words and the Gospel of Jesus, which tells us to do unto the least of these. It is not true to Isaiah's telling us that the plumb line is righteousness.

Living plumb doesn't mean that life will always be pleasant. To remain true may mean some shifting foundation moves us off of plumb, and we may we need to be tapped back in to plumb or rebraced. It maybe even requires a good whack with a holy sledgehammer. Still the true will be right for us. As Jenifer Faulkner says,

About a dozen years ago I became critically ill and I have a vivid memory of looking down on myself on the bed; doctors and nurses worked on that body, and I felt held in such secureness, joy and contentment, a sense of the utter rightness of things—I was held in the hands of God. The crisis passed and I was filled with wonder at the newness of life.

A sense of the utter rightness of things and those things being held in God is why "How is this true?" is an essential query.

Testing for True _____

Relax your body, mind, and spirit.

Take two or three deep breaths.

Put the book down and think about the following slowly and gently.

Has there been a time in my life in the midst of difficulty that what was happening felt utterly true and right? What made it feel that way?

We want to be right in the best sense of that word while being held by God. Building true on the foundation of God's love, grace, and truth is essential. It is like the story that Jesus tells of two builders.

> Therefore everyone who hears these words of mine and puts them into practice is like a wise man who built his house on the rock. The rain came down, the streams rose, and the winds blew and beat against that house; yet it did not fall, because it had its foundation on the rock. But everyone who hears these words of mine and does not put them into practice is like a foolish man who built his house on sand. The rain came down, the streams rose, and the winds blew and beat against that house, and it fell with a great crash.

If we listen to the divine Word, put that word into practice doing the work that we are meant to do—not could do, ought to do, but are meant to do—there will be that sense of utter rightness, a work that is true in all ways and able to withstand all storms.

True to Our Lives

In the same way that our timber frame, when assembled correctly, was true, the true that matters to us in our vocations, relationships, and very lives is the true that fits with where we are. At each stage of building the timber frame, each piece had to be set in its correct place so that the next piece could follow and hold together in integrity. The pieces had come together in the right order, each piece building on the ones before. Otherwise, the frame would have been a haphazard disaster not fit for anything.

So too with our lives. Each piece builds on the next. And while each may be true in its time, the final trueness is not seen until completeness is achieved. That's something few of us see this side of eternity.

Still, seeking plumb takes us to our true selves. Saint Catherine of Siena says, "If you are what you should be, you will set the whole world ablaze!" I would say that if you are what you should be—what you were created to be—you will set your self ablaze. Ablaze with the light you need to truly live. To truly be the person God created you to be.

Likewise, if you aren't what you should be, you'll not only not set the world ablaze—you'll put your own fire out. We are not mass-produced robots from some heavenly factory—all programmed alike to do exactly the same things. Yet, at times, we seem to think that this individuality that we're created with is not the ideal and that the will of God is to shape us into something we're not. God created us to be the individuals we are. To think that God wants to force us into that which we were not created to be will, at the very least, stunt our growth into the very people God created us to be. At the worst, it could kill our souls and our will to live as a people of God.

Testing for True _____

Relax your body, mind, and spirit.

Take two or three deep breaths.

Put the book down and think about the following slowly and gently.

How is not living true to the person I feel God created me to be hindering my spiritual life? My daily life?

As a kid growing in an Evangelical Quaker congregation, I attended (or was made to go, depending on who you asked, me or my parents) a number of presentations by missionaries home on furlough. These earnest, dedicated folks who had just come back from India, Taiwan, or East Africa told harrowing stories, which I found thrilling. They ended almost every service with a plea for the young people in our church to join them. They asked us to pray about doing that. While I mostly enjoyed hearing about their adventures, I never did pray such a prayer. I was afraid to. I admired them, but even as a kid, it didn't feel like the path for me. I was certain that if I prayed about being a missionary, God would say, "Brent, go to" someplace I didn't want to go regardless of my deepest feelings that being a missionary was not for me.

My first mistake, I see now, was not understanding that their calls fit their lives. Their lives might have been hard at times, but they found joy in what they were doing because that's what they were meant to do. My second mistake was thinking that my call would not fit the life I felt deeply in my being, even if I couldn't articulate it back then, that I should live. That's why I now resonate with Parker J. Palmer's statement that the

true self is the self with which we arrive on earth, the self that simply wants us to be who we were born to be. True self tells us who we are, where we are planted in the ecosystem of life, what "right action" looks like for us, and how we can grow more fully into our own potentials.

God made me to be me! What a glorious thought.
What a glorious thought indeed.
That's not to say God won't stretch and grow and change me as I move through life. That's happened throughout my life—growth opportunities abound. Some pleasant. Some not. That also doesn't mean God won't call me to do something I'm not inclined to do. That has also happened. It does mean that whatever I'm called to do will be true to my nature as conceived by God. Aquinas has a proposition about this in which he says, "For a stone is called true, which possesses the nature proper to a stone." I use this particular quote for two reasons. One is that, sadly, I sometimes don't grasp the nature proper to a John Brent Bill. The second is, the stone—which most of us consider nonsentient—does. That's something Jesus seemed to recognize when the Pharisees begged him to still his disciples' shouting praises as he entered Jerusalem. "'I tell you,' he replied, 'if they keep quiet, the stones will cry out.'"

Perhaps stones (and trees and flowers and dirt) recognize their nature as part of God's good creation better than we do. I say this as a person who deals with nature on a regular basis. Throughout the woods here, there are five different varieties of oak tree. Some have been planted from saplings a year old. Others have sprung up voluntarily from acorns that have been dropped. Each grows into its type of oak tree. It is oak tree true. It does not become a maple, a crabapple, a Kentucky coffee tree, or any of the other types of trees around it. It "listens," if you will, to what it's called to be and grows in that direction.

Testing for True _____

Relax your body, mind, and spirit.

Take two or three deep breaths.

Put the book down and think about the following slowly and gently.

In what ways do I live true to the essence of my soul and nature as created by God?

To know our truest selves, it is important that we listen to what our lives are saying to us. My friend the poet and priest Catharine Phillips reminds me of that in her poem "Voice."

> Some days
> Like this one
> I have to stay away
> From other voices
> So I can hear my own,
> Find the part that connects,
> The rhizome underground
> Like the lily of the valley
> Behind the garage.
> It still finds its way
> Through the dirt
> Behind the last remaining peony.
> I forget there are flowers
> Back there
> Unless I remember

Unless I take the time
To look.
The lily of the valley has now moved
Underground
Behind the last remaining peony.
It has moved, yes,
But remains true.
Soon it will sing its particular fragrance,
No matter who is listening.

When we learn to listen to our truest self, then we begin to live "plumb right."

Does the Church Support or Hinder Us in Living True?

I've been thinking about that question for decades now. Is the community of faith on our side (and God's!) as we endeavor to live into our true selves? Or is it more concerned with maintaining itself?

Hopefully, our best and most faithful congregations care about and facilitate our finding our true selves and the work we're called to do. Faith communities need to nurture us in ways that help us see the movements of the Holy Spirit in our lives. They should encourage us to explore faithful living by using our gifts and talents in ways that feel right to us. And give us opportunities to do so.

But, alas, I have too often experienced congregations that were more concerned with me doing the right things as they defined right and with filling their needs instead of mine. Or God's. Some words by Thomas Kelly helped clarify my feeling for me:

I wish I might emphasize how a life becomes simplified when dominated by faithfulness to a few concerns. Too many of us have too many irons in the fire. We get distracted by the intellectual claim to our interest in a thousand and one good things, and before we know it we are pulled and hauled breathlessly along by an over-burdened program of good committees and good undertakings. I am persuaded that this fevered life of church workers is not wholesome. Undertakings get plastered on from the outside because we can't turn down a friend. Acceptance of service on a weighty committee should really depend upon an answering imperative within us, not merely upon a rational calculation of the factors involved. The concern-orientated life is ordered and organized from within. And we learn to say No as well as Yes by attending to the guidance of inner responsibility.

That short passage is so packed full of truth. Let's start with where he says, "we are pulled and hauled breathlessly along by an over-burdened program of good committees and good undertakings." Wow. Is that not a description of why many of us duck when we see somebody from our congregation's nominating committee or religious education committee or any committee heading our way?

Perhaps that ducking is why some British Quakers came up with a card game titled "Unable, Unwilling." "Unable, Unwilling" is a satirical game based on Friends' nominating processes, which, while they have our special Quaker quirks, are recognizable to members of most any congregation or religious organization. Each player draws cards and does her best to nominate other players to committees and positions. Some of these positions really exist in Quaker meetings' structure, like clerk or treasurer. Others poke fun at our supposed leanings (representative to Quaker Concern for Random Left-Wing Causes) or are downright silly (Solidarity with Antarctic Friends Committee rep.).

Each position or committee appointment comes with a certain number of stress points. Once you've collected fifteen stress points, you've got committee burnout and lost the game.

The good news is that there are cards you might draw that let you fend off a nomination by pleading overwork or by nominating the "worthy Friend" to one side of you, and so forth.

The game, while fun, raises holy questions about how we can, with integrity, get out of serving on "good committees and good undertakings" if they're not good and true for us. The work may be good. But if we find ourselves drained from being pulled and hauled breathlessly along, they might not be good for us. No matter how important the work is. If we come home late at night from our "good" committee meetings and drop exhaustedly into bed, then Kelly is right when he says, "I am persuaded that this fevered life of church workers is not wholesome."

Indeed. And I would add, exhaustion, feeling discouraged or disheartened, or feeling ready to quit are further signs that perhaps we're not in the work or committee that's right for us. It's not true to our life.

Testing for True _____

Relax your body, mind, and spirit.

Take two or three deep breaths.

Put the book down and think about the following slowly and gently.

Have I ever said yes to something good and worthy that I wanted to say no to because it didn't feel right and true for me to do? What might I have done in such an instance that would have been truer to my life?

Jesus's life, while filled to the brim and more, was not fevered in the way we hear his disciples today complaining theirs is. Perhaps that's because the work we're offered is work that needs done but is not ultimately life-giving or true to our individual talents, inclinations, ministry, or mission. Jesus stayed focused on his mission. He did not, so far as we know, serve on his local synagogue's building and grounds committee. He didn't agree to be one of the ushers on High Holy Days.

Kelly is spot on when he says that we're interested in a thousand and one good things. There are a thousand and one good things that need doing. There were in Jesus's time too. But Jesus's example shows that his life, amid that call to thousands of things (think of when Satan tempted him), was that he stayed true to his life and call. His life was simplified by sticking faithfully to the concerns that were his. By staying centered on being true to his ministry and mission, he lived a life whose integrity was recognized by all who witnessed him moving through life. He exemplified the truth of Proverbs 11:3: "The integrity of the upright guides them."

Jesus did the work he came to this life to do. That's an example we need to follow—and encourage our congregations to consider. What is the work to which we're called, with the interests and skills to do it? Not for a set number of terms based on a book of discipline or order, but from a sense of mission and purpose. Our faith communities need to find ways to help us live faithfully and truly to our callings.

One of the key truths of Kelly's passage is when he writes about accepting service depending "upon an answering imperative within us, not merely upon a rational calculation of the factors involved." Again, I posit that the answering imperative is fourfold—Are beauty, truth, life, and love each present in the answering imperative? If they are, then it is ours to do.

Especially, so far as this chapter is concerned, truth. To know what is true for our life at this time, we need to listen to what our life is saying. I know I've mentioned this before, but it can be especially important when the nominating committee, well intentioned as they are, approaches. If you're sick to your stomach at the thought of a particular position—listen to your body. If you think, "Oh no, not that committee"—listen to your head. If you feel, "Wow, that sounds grand"—listen to your feelings.

Of course, it's best when your feelings, head, heart, and soul are all in alignment saying "*Yes!*"

Testing for True _____

Relax your body, mind, and spirit.

Take two or three deep breaths.

Put the book down and think about the following slowly and gently.

How do I know whether to listen to my head or my feelings in determining what's true for me to do?

The Jesuit Herbert Alphonso, in *Discovering Your Personal Vocation*, writes,

> Before I can tell my life what I want to do with it, I must listen to my life telling me who I am. I must listen for the truths and values at the heart of my own identity, not the standards by which I must live—but the standards by which I cannot help but live if I am living my own life.
>
> Only after we listen—and continue listening as we go through life—to our life telling us who we are will we be able to live true to the life we were meant to live. Once we learn to continually listen to what our life is saying, we will be well on our way to living a life that is ordered and organized by truth—the truth within us planted by the Holy Spirit. And we will be able to deflect good nominations in favor of the right nomination.

How the True Might Change Over Our Lives

I referred earlier to the timber frame of my house being erected in a certain way—each post and beam being numbered and going in a specific order and place. How each built on the one that went before. Our lives are like that. But unlike the timber frame that had to be fully complete before any other construction on the house began, our lives are works in progress. While each experience builds on the ones that went before, our lives may well shift in ways that my house frame better not! Staying true for us does not mean being rigid. In fact, rigidity might cause us to snap when presented with fresh movement of the Holy Spirit in our lives. We need to be flexible. In that way we're more like an oak tree than we are a timber frame. An oak tree changes. From acorn to seedling to sapling to mature tree. Throughout its life it remains true to being an oak, yet it changes. It must, or it is no longer true to its nature. Another thing the oak tree shows us is that what is true for the acorn is not true for the fully formed tree—or the stages in between the two.

In that same way, what is true for us in our youth and in old age might be vastly different. I'd be surprised if it wasn't. Which is why we must learn to be true to the age we are—our stage of life.

In my own life, I know that many of the relationships that were vital in my teen years wouldn't be true for the age I am now. Not because they were bad but because I (and the people I was in relationship with then) am a vastly different person than I was then. The same is true of the jobs I held then. Running a go-kart track was great fun when I was sixteen. It might be great fun now—for a day or so. And while that sixteen-year-old go-kart-track operator dreamt of being a writer, he wasn't at the place in his life where he could do it effectively, helpfully, or well. He had neither the temperament nor the ability to be a good writer. Likewise, my older body doesn't really feel up to sitting on the ground for prolonged periods of time tuning up one-cylinder gas engines or replacing broken-down seats. Heck, I'm the one with a broken-down seat now.

That is why it is important to consider, in relationships, vocations, and discernment, how these things fit with my life as it is and as it is becoming. Reflecting on what your life experiences up until now have taught you can help with this. They can show how something is, or isn't, true to who you are now.

As I look over my life and see when I really listened to my true self, I see times when my education, talents, age, and more all aligned for the position or relationship I was entering. Those supremely sublime moments are too rare in my life (partly because I'm a slow learner), but when they have happened they have resulted in satisfying and spiritual growth experiences.

Testing for True

Relax your body, mind, and spirit.

Take two or three deep breaths.

Put the book down and think about the following slowly and gently.

What are things I can do to help me determine if something is true for my life now? Or continues to be true to my life now?

Another thing I've learned is that, in addition to knowing when the time is right to enter something, I also need to be aware of when it's time to leave. Many things in our lives are not good for the whole of our lives. That is especially true, I think, in ministry situations.

I've known far too many people who felt a call to a particular ministry and felt it was for all their life. For some it was. My observation is, however, that many lifelong calls to ministry manifest themselves in various forms of ministry over a lifetime. Youth ministry. Pastoral ministry. Denominational ministry. Chaplaincy. I've also observed that if a person stays in the same place or ministry for a long, long time, she or he risks not being able to see when it no longer fits the truth of their life. Then they become ineffective and unhappy and frustrated.

I'm not saying that's true in every case. I know a sizable number of people who have spent their lives in the same type of ministry. Some even in the same congregation or organization.

What I am saying is that it is a danger if we don't learn to stay attuned to the truth of where we are and who we are. A danger that could harm us and whatever we're engaged in. If we are being true to where we are, then God gives us the power to be faithful, effective, and helpful.

Falseness

In the same way that we need to look for what is true, we must also learn to recognize what is no longer completely true or has even become false.

I learned that lesson well when I worked as a "circuit rider" for the Indiana Association of United Ways. My job was to help seed new community fund organizations in small, rural counties that did not have one. It was challenging and fulfilling work. But it also kept me on the road for most work weeks. I drove at least six hundred miles a week, ate in restaurants, and lived in hotels. After five years of such intense work, my body started trying to tell me something. It did so via a variety of signals. At first, I ignored them.

The signals started with panic attacks. Now panic attacks were something I'd dealt with for years. But they usually came in times of lots of stress. Then they started occurring weekly. Soon they were happening almost daily.

Another signal that I ignored is that I was irritable most of the time. I was pleasant or even fun to be with in public, but in private, including with my family and staff members, I wasn't nearly so nice. Folks avoided me.

Other body signs included being thirsty constantly, putting on weight, and my vision changing rapidly.

I didn't like myself or life very much.

Finally, I spoke to a good friend who was also my family physician. He ran one test and informed me that I had diabetes. My blood sugars were so out of control that I was in danger of having a stroke. Through education, diet, exercise, and good medicines, I began to get the diabetes regulated. But it was hard with a grueling schedule, eating out all the time, and sleeping in hotels. Though I loved the job when I started it and it fit my life at that time, it no longer did. Not if I wanted to live—let alone live abundantly. And so it became clear that I should look for something that required less travel and had less stress. For something that would fit my new health normal.

In God's timing, since I was finally listening for what was true instead of pushing against that which had become false, a perfect opportunity to serve came along. One that utilized my skills, required no overnight travel, and fit with my new regimen for regaining physical and emotional health.

Plumb was restored. I was back to living the words of Frederick Douglass that "I prefer to be true to myself, even at the hazard of incurring the ridicule of others, rather than to be false, and to incur my own abhorrence." I began to like life—and myself—once again.

Testing for True _____

Relax your body, mind, and spirit.

Take two or three deep breaths.

Put the book down and think about the following slowly and gently.

What signals do I get from my body, head, or soul that something is no longer true to my life and that it's time for some kind of change? How do I recognize signs of falseness?

Of course, discovering when something is no longer true doesn't necessarily mean having the seismic signs of panic attacks or chronic disease. No, our bodily or emotional or spiritual signals are often subtler than that. Sometimes, at least at first, they may be so subtle that they are hard to sense.

Photography is something I enjoy. One autumn day while kicking around North Hero Island, Vermont, camera in hand, I came across an abandoned old house that was slowly falling apart. Its weathered wood, paint stripped by the winds off Lake Champlain, and crazy angles as it began collapsing made for great photographs. Doors hung askew in frames they no longer fit. Window frames were now malformed, cracking the glass panes as they shifted. I wondered—When did the people who lived there notice the shifts? Was it when the first door no longer closed tight and the howling lake winds began making their way into the house? Or was it when wisps of snow gathered in the inside corners of windows that didn't hang as straight as they had when the house was built? How long did the people who lived there stay in a home that was no longer comfortable because it was no longer true?

Did they stay because it was familiar and moving might be hard?

Did they try to retrue the house by fixing the foundation where needed?

Those questions could be asked of our lives. Do we notice the sagging foundations of our lives? The doors that don't close right?

Testing Whether It's True

If we want to live with integrity to our truest selves, then there are some things we can do to test our leadings, vocations, relationships, and so on.

One is to ask four basic, but important questions:

- How does it fit my current circumstances?
- How does it fit my education or training?
- How does it fit my financial situation?
- How does it fit my family situation?

Let's look at each of these.

First, How does it fit my current circumstances? This is a big question. It ties in with what I said earlier about being true to the seasons of our lives and how they change us. First, we need to look at our current circumstances. While that seems more than a little obvious, most of us are so busy living that we rarely stop to examine our lives and what circumstances constitute it. Such an examination of our circumstances will help us see if our leadings and so on are true to our lives. By current circumstances I mean things as seemingly ordinary as where we live, our ability to move to a new location if needed, our place in our jobs (just starting out, nearing retirement), our physical health, or how important our current faith communities are to us and us to them.

All of these can help us determine whether where we are at this point is the place we need to be—or stay. Or if this "new thing" is right for us.

Next, How does it fit my education or training? I mentioned earlier how I have wanted to be a writer since I was a young person but that back then I wasn't in the place to be effective or helpful. That's because, while I had the desire, I had no training in being a writer. I was a voracious reader; which writers need to be. I was a storyteller. I was funny. But I had no training in how to write for publication. I didn't know the basics about how to craft a short story, a humor piece, or any of the things I wanted to write.

Eventually, after taking some creative writing classes in college and graduate school, I acquired the skills to help my desire become reality. Much to the dismay of editors and readers everywhere.

How does it fit my financial situation? This might sound like a pretty cold and calculating sort of question, devoid of spirituality. It's not. Asking, Can I afford to follow this leading? helps us unpack a myriad of things. Among those might be whether it is an unrealistic desire I have because I'm trapped in a job I hate and I want to do something else. Anything else! Whether it's true to me or not.

Another thing my answer to this question might reveal is whether my financial resources are solid enough for now to be the right time to invest them in what I feel called to. This question can also help me consider, if I don't have the necessary resources but still feel that this is true leading, whether I have the wherewithal to raise the needed funds without going into debt. Do I have the drive and skills necessary to do so?

The final question is, How does it fit my family situation? I often joke about the early Quaker missionaries who had large families and left them to travel in ministry. Did they really have a leading to a valid ministry, or did they just want to get away from all those kids? This is a serious question, though. If you have family, you have to consider how following a leading will affect them. Is this leading or job consistent with your having family responsibilities at this time? Are your family members in unity with what you're feeling?

I was once asked to consider a position in a certain city and at a particular institution. When I mentioned it to Nancy, she said, "I hope you'll be very happy there." While she was joking (I think), it did make me stop and think. I knew she didn't like that town. Nor did she care for some parts of the position that I'd be stepping into. Since I had a commitment to her, I had to take that commitment into consideration as I pondered whether this was for me.

I also had to consider her wisdom and how well she knew me. She knew I would not be happy there for a number of reasons.

So, I said no.

Shortly after that, I was offered a position that was a good fit for both of us and our extended family. This helped to remind me that my being true to the life God created me to have is not a solitary endeavor. To live my truest life, I have to take into consideration those I'm in relationship with personally, professionally, financially, and so on if it's to be really true.

The questions above aren't the only ones we should ask. They're starting places. They are important, however. As you contemplate them, other questions that are true and specific to you will come. As will answers, from God as you pray and listen silently, from Scripture, from trusted spiritual friends, and from the truth in your soul speaking to you.

Testing for True _____

Relax your body, mind, and spirit.

Take two or three deep breaths.

Put the book down and think about the following slowly and gently.

Are there questions I can ask that are particular to my life that will help me assess whether something is true to my life?

The writer Wayne Muller says:

> The truth is never far from your heart and your spirit. Every person you touch, every act of kindness, every gesture born of your love can uncover something deeply true within and around you. And with each act of truthfulness, you touch a deeper chord in yourself and others. As Emerson said, "Our life is an apprenticeship to truth, that around every circle another can be drawn . . . under every deep a lower deep opens."

I love this quote because it says a lot about the plumb truth I've been talking about. A truth that fits with who we are. A truth that comes from God's Spirit working within us to bring out the persons God created us to be. The truth that is never far from our hearts and our spirits and our bodies—the deep trueness of our lives—reveals itself in acts of love, joy, peace, forbearance, kindness, goodness, faithfulness, gentleness, and self-control. Such things are indicators of the abundant life Jesus says he came to bring us.

Muller's quotation also exemplifies how beauty, truth, life, and love are integrated. Living true results in acts of love. Acts of love create beauty. Beauty gives us life. Life is truly what we were created to experience.

Beauty. Truth. Life. Love. The Möbius strip of faith—never ending, winding from one to the next, in harmony.

Experiencing a sense of the utter rightness of things and those things being held in God is why "How is this true"? is an essential spiritual question. Answering that question prayerfully and truthfully adds to the beauty of our lives just as the clear, level light of a late autumn afternoon shines gold on everything it touches.

CHAPTER 4

Life—Vim, Vigor, and Vivacity

———

You make known to me the path of life.
—PSALM 16:11

Life is the art of drawing without an eraser.
—JOHN W. GARDNER

Life. From our first squalling breath as a baby, we cling to it. Our bodies sense that we were made for life. When we are sick or injured, we seek healing so that our life can continue. When I was rushed to the hospital with congestive heart failure and pneumonia a couple of years ago, I relished every clear whiff of oxygen flowing through the tubes to my nose. I wasn't, surprisingly to me, afraid of dying. I did want to live, however. Life called to me.

The will to live is so strong that sometimes, even when bodies and minds are failing and so-called life-support systems are switched off, some of us live on, clasping on to that force that animates us in this world.

It is not just we humans who seek life. As I write this, it is late autumn. I hear the sandhill cranes' plaintive cries as they soar south at three thousand feet high on their five-foot wingspans, their long legs trailing behind them, headed for the warmer climes of Florida. I also spy squirrel nests. I witness the disappearance of the fallen walnuts that littered the ground just a few weeks ago, now safely stored for squirrelly sustenance for the winter that's coming to Indiana.

We animals are not the only beings on earth that seek life. As I walk through my prairie, I see tree seedlings sprouting from seeds dropped by birds or in the scat of mammals. When I go to the city in the summer, I glimpse dandelions and tufts of grass popping up through tiny cracks in sidewalks and streets.

When I behold all this, I am reminded of the creation stories in Genesis. In those accounts, everything is created to sustain life. It doesn't matter whether you believe these are literal accounts of how the world came into being or metaphors showing how God brought life via the big bang or other evolutionary methods. These stories reveal God as the one who created us and all things for life.

Many of us move through life taking part in life-giving activities. From farmers raising crops to doctors performing organ transplants to teachers educating the life of the mind and artists of all stripes bringing us beauty. We run food banks to feed the hungry, build hospitals to heal the sick, plant prairies to feed the butterflies and birds and renew the earth, recycle plastic, and so much more.

We do that when we are walking close to the people we were created to be, that is. At times, though, we humans get twisted and work toward death. Perhaps we think that doing so will preserve our life or the way we think life should be. That's how holocausts, mass murders, Auschwitzes, pogroms, racial hatred, class divisions, drone bombings, and hateful, mean social policies come into being.

Sadly, it seems that we humans alone among all created beings are capable of such horrors.

In lesser ways, when we forget that we were created for life, we engage in activities or actions that lead us away from life. This is not a big lecture on avoiding smoking, drinking, and all the other things my evangelical upbringing preached against. Nor am I going to address not using salt, staying away from fatty foods and sugars, and other things that my cardiologist and endocrinologist warn me about. And they, though they did not grow up in the kind of church I did, agree with the anti-smoking-and-drinking part!

But I am aware, especially in retrospect, of things I've chosen to do, despite warnings, that could shorten my physical life. I make fewer bad choices now. That's in no small part because while I don't see the exact time of the end of my days, I know that time is much closer than it was when I was young and invincible. And so I treasure each day and tend to the things such as eating healthy, exercising, taking my medicines, and so forth that help lengthen, not shorten, my life.

But just as deadly as physical choices I've made, so too are those things I've done that sucked spiritual or emotional life out of me. Those are choices I made to do things that did not renew my spirit, did not lead me beside the still waters of refreshment and communion with God, and decreased my feeling that I was truly living.

Some of those things were good things. It's just that they weren't good for me. It's hard to argue that serving on an important congregational committee or helping at a food bank could be a bad thing—something not life-giving. However, we've all experienced things that were good and worthy, yet that still sucked the life out of us.

I'm not speaking here of things that just made us tired or were difficult. I'm talking about work or relationships that left us drained of all life—physically, emotionally, mentally, and spirituality. We need to say no to things that drain life out of us. We need to remember that we were created for life. When we look for what is ours to do, we need to seek that which brings life.

Life Lines _____

Relax your body, mind, and spirit.

Take two or three deep breaths.

Put the book down and think about the following slowly and gently.

How often do I choose things that give me life? What are things that tell me something is or isn't life-giving?

If we, who call ourselves the friends of Jesus, want to live the abundant life that he promises, both collectively and as individuals, we will ask of all our actions, Will this bring life?

Vim

Vim is one of my favorite words, even if I don't use it much. *Merriam-Webster* defines it as "robust energy and enthusiasm." Synonyms for *vim* include *beans, gas, get-up-and-go, zing, zip,* and many more. My grandad used to accuse me of being full of beans. I don't think he meant vim, though I certainly had more physical energy back then than I do today.

Even now, as I age, I have a good deal of vim for certain things. Key relationships. Walking in the prairie. Listening to good music. Leading workshops. Reading well-written books. Writing. Photography. Driving my old MG. Others may judge some of these things as more important or worthy than others. But they are each life-giving to me. They feed my spirit, enliven my soul, and add joy to my daily ordinary life.

As I think about my feeling called to a ministry of writing, which first started almost forty years ago, the "Will this bring life?" question continues to be answered with an unqualified yes.

That's not to say writing isn't hard. It is. At least for me. I know it's easier for some others. Once when I was teaching writing at Earlham School of Religion, I invited another Quaker author to make a presentation on his writing life. "Writing is easy," he began. After four weeks of my telling the class just how hard it was, I was furious—in a very Friendly way, of course. A way I call pacifist-aggressive.

Later, as we talked, I discovered that writing truly *was* easy for him. I was surprised. But not envious. I need it to be hard. That way I must take my time and be care-full of the process.

Unlike my friend, I don't just sit down and start writing. I write. I pace. I fuss. I rewrite. I question myself. I question my editor's wisdom in asking me to author the book or article I'm working on. I write some more. I vacuum the rug. I think. I write.

For me writing is almost as hard as spending a day splitting wood. The difference is, I really don't enjoy splitting wood. I don't find it particularly life-giving. It's a chore that needs to be done, though.

My dad, unlike me, loved splitting wood—and everything that went with it. He loved to get out the big chainsaw, hook up the splitter to the tractor, and spend the day outdoors turning cut-up logs into firewood. I preferred to sit on the porch with an engaging book and watch him split wood. I didn't sit on the porch and watch him, of course, but that's what I wanted to do.

That's not to say I hate splitting wood. After the first few satisfying splits, however, its initial invigorating enthusiasm has worn off. I know I'll enjoy that split wood when I see it stacked up along the driveway or in the woodshed, ready for me to bring in for a fire that will warm our house, bodies, and souls. But soon after I start splitting, I begin calculating how many more logs are still to be placed in the splitter, how many splits each log will take depending on its size, and how long it'll be before I'll be able to take a nice warm shower. And maybe a nap.

That's the difference between how my dad and I saw splitting wood. He found it invigorating. He enjoyed the roar of the chainsaw, stacking the wood so it could dry, building bonfires to burn up the small limbs he'd trimmed off the bigger logs.

One of my favorite pictures of Dad is of him sitting on the ground as night falls. His white hair shines in the light of the fire he'd started at the end of a long day, bright sparks from the fire flitting up into the darkening sky. It's a portrait of a man completely content after hard, good work. He was tired physically, but his soul was enriched and filled with life from how he'd spent his day.

After I snapped his picture, he looked over at me. "This is living," he smiled. And it was for him.

That's how I feel at the end of a day of writing. For all its demanding work, I am tired, but invigorated. It gives me life—the intellectual wrestling with how to bring an idea to life so my readers will "get" what I mean in a meaningful way.

Writing gives me life. Now before you think I'm painting some picture of the writer's life that is all sweetness and light with Disneyesque bunnies, chipmunks, and deer looking on admiringly while a flaxen-haired beautiful muse whispers inspiration into my ear, let me say that it's not. Not every moment of writing is completely life-giving if taken individually. Some are, like when I find just the right word, a sentence finally flows, or I hold my first copy of my new book. Other times, I must push through, knowing that, in the end, as a whole, the hard work will have been life-giving. It will be my version of sitting by the bonfire, as words and thoughts flit up into the sky, as did Dad's sparks.

Life Lines _____

Relax your body, mind, and spirit.

Take two or three deep breaths.

Put the book down and think about the following slowly and gently.

What is something that is hard but that still energizes me? Why or how does it add vitality to my life?

In addition to being life-giving for me, my writing, I've also found, gives life to others. Most often these others are people I don't know personally and never will. Regardless, I am grateful that many readers find what I write helpful or comforting or challenging in some significant way. And at times I even get to meet someone my writing has touched. Or I get an e-mail or letter such as the one I received that said, "I just wanted to write you and share with you how your book has changed my life. . . . I thank God for you and your ministry to my spirit." God, in God's grace-filled wisdom, allowed my writing to make its way to David, who's a Pentecostal pastor in a state far from mine. That little book led us both to life, though in quite different ways. Missives like David's help confirm, by their life-giving nature, that the ministry of writing is a calling for me.

We often forget that life gives life. Perhaps that's why the God of life calls us to life. When we forget that, we then begin to think that living in God's will for us leads to a life of drudgery and drain. The opposite is true. It may be difficult, but it won't be wearisome. If what we're truly called to do is from God, even if it's hard, it will give life, not steal it. That is true for the entirety of our lives—regardless of age, health, spiritual maturity, or any other factor.

That's why I love the optimistic tone of something Quaker William Littleboy wrote:

> Here is the unfailing attraction of the life in Christ. It is a life which even to old age, is always on the upgrade; there is always something calling for a joyful looking forward; it is a life where, across each revelation of God's grace as it comes to us is written, in letters of gold, Thou shalt see greater things than these. It gives full scope . . . to our desire for high adventure. No conceivable life can be so interesting, so stimulating, as that which we live in Christ.

I especially like that "even to old age" part. That season of my life is drawing near. Okay, it's here. Still, it is good to know that my spiritual adventure won't be ending just because I've reached geezer-hood.

If Littleboy's words are true, and I'm finding they are, then I have the promise of living abundantly, with divine assistance, until I die. Daily life and the things I'm called to do will be life-giving, even if they're different from the things I did in my earlier stages of life. Littleboy's words, along with those I read in the Bible and those that God speaks in my soul, tell me that there is still much to achieve in my life. Things that will do more than merely sustain me physically, but that will give me life emotionally, mentally, and spiritually.

I equally like Littleboy's statement "It gives full scope . . . to our desire for high adventure. No conceivable life can be so interesting, so stimulating, as that which we live in Christ."

Yes!

I still desire high adventure. The adventure that I want is different in significant ways from that which I wanted when I was younger. As a young kid, I wanted to be a cowboy or a firefighter or a pilot. Later, I wanted to be race-car driver. I don't think I'm unusual in desiring adventure. There is something in us that craves adventure. That finds it life-giving. Hence my dad's love of roller coasters; the late George H. W. Bush's skydiving at ages seventy-five, eighty, and ninety; my friend Katrina's scuba diving; my youngest sister's whitewater-rafting expeditions; and more. Undertaking an exploration of something new, be it of a deep, dark cave or the spiritual exploration of our souls, can be equally life-giving, depending on the person.

That doesn't mean adventure is always fun or easy. It can be hard. And scary. Like the time I strapped into a two-seater Dallara Indy Car behind Felipe Giaffone for high-speed laps around the two-and-a-half-mile track at the Indianapolis Motor Speedway. After signing a ream of legal papers, I was ushered into a dressing room where I stripped off my jeans and golf shirt and was fitted with a Nomex racing suit and fire-retardant racing shoes. Fire retardant! Obviously, I was not going to be tooling around the track in my Toyota.

After an instruction session, and just before climbing into the car, I donned a fire-retardant balaclava, racing gloves, suit, and helmet. Once in the car, I was snugged into place with a four-point racing harness and neck restraint. This was serious equipment for a serious situation.

Screaming into turn three at 180 miles per hour gave me new insight into high adventure and life. Just a few seconds earlier, we had rocketed out of the pits and up onto the track. Now we were hurtling toward the turn. Giaffone ran up through the gears gaining speed every second. As we neared the turn, my vision dimmed. I'd been holding my breath ever since he'd taken off!

It was then I realized that I could either fret myself into a heart attack or I trust that the guy in front of me was skilled and that this was going to be among the most exciting times of my life.

So, I prayed a prayer of trust in Giaffone and the laws of physics that glued the race car to the track, took a breath, relaxed my tense muscles, and watched the track surface, walls, trees, and viewing stands come and go in less than the blink of an eye.

In under two minutes we'd made our two laps around the track and were pulling back into the pits. I climbed up and out of the car and walked shakily toward safety behind the pit wall. I'd been scared breathless but was feeling fully alive. Pictures of that moment show my face lit up and wearing a smile that wraps around my head.

Now, of course, no one could experience that kind of euphoria every day. Life is just not that way. But still, there should be a certain constant joy in our lives—the joy that comes from walking with God. That's part of the adventure God takes us on. A life with God is fraught with possible danger, sprinkled with moments of sheer beauty and amazement, and punctuated by long periods of sameness—like being strapped into the tiny cockpit of a speeding car bouncing over tarmac, fighting G-forces, muscle strain, and thirty-two other drivers for five hundred miles.

Five miles was enough for me. But for people like Giaffone, it's not.

Despite the dangers, my fast laps were a completely overwhelming experience, filled with deep joy. Giaffone was a pro and had every intention of giving me the ride of my life while bringing me safely to the finish line. Like the life of faith. Christ brings us home safely if we trust that we are to live with vim in all our endeavors.

Life Lines

Relax your body, mind, and spirit.

Take two or three deep breaths.

Put the book down and think about the following slowly and gently.

Have I ever had an adventure that was scary but made me feel fully alive at the same time? What were the hallmarks of that experience? Where was God in it?

Someday I believe it will be abundantly clear that, for all our doubts in this life, angels have been watching over us, O Lord. If we are willing to see them in our midst, we will get the messages and go on the adventures that God meant us to have. From then on we will live the lives our life-giving God wants us to live. All our life! Then, someday, in that great land to which we all travel, we will see our angels and slap our spiritual foreheads and say, "That was living! What's next?"

Vigor

Vigor is another good "life" word. Sources say it is derived from the Old French *vigour*, which in turn came from Latin *vigor*, from *vigere*, "be lively." I think that we'd all agree that to be lively is a good thing. The question is how to stay lively.

We often forget, in our endeavors to do the divine will, to look for life. Yet Jesus himself said, "I am the way and the truth and the life," and "I came so that they might have life and have it more abundantly." Hmmm, might we translate that last one as "I have come that they may have life and have it vigorously"? Probably not and be faithful to the text, but I'll do it anyway.

When I think about *vigor* and its root of "be lively," I also recall times when life seemed to lose that quality. I've discovered, and you have as well, that something that starts out life-giving doesn't necessarily stay that way. But too often we—or I, at least—are oblivious to when it ceases to be life-giving. Instead it becomes life-draining. As much as I hate to admit it, sometimes I'm unwilling to see what should be obvious.

That happened to me in a very big way many years ago. I had accepted a position at an important, newly founded not-for-profit in Indianapolis. Its mission fit with things I deeply believed in. My skills, talents, and interests matched the organization's needs. It turned out to be a good match for many years. I got to use my design and communications abilities, helped develop important policies and procedures, worked with interesting people, and utilized my undergraduate art degree when I chose art and furniture for our new offices. This was the position I referred to in chapter 1.

As the years went by, the organization grew. As did my role. New staff were added. This included people to do some of the work I had enjoyed. New offices were set up around the state. Our program offerings expanded.

These were good things. They showed that we were meeting our mission and truly helping the people and places we were meant to serve. It was satisfying to see this work maturing and knowing I'd had a hand in it.

However, my role became increasingly administrative and less and less interactive with folks outside the organization. I missed seeing clients, printers, art gallery owners, staff in other similar organizations around the United States, and more. Don't get me wrong—I loved the people I worked with. I still do. I was also competent in the position and making positive contributions. And I was making a substantial salary with wonderful benefits. I was doing good and worthy work.

But much of the liveliness I originally experienced was gone. Sitting in an office going over tax forms, budgets, personnel annual reviews; preparing reports for board meetings; and the like didn't have the same invigorating quality as seeing a new publication take shape or visiting a client and spending a couple of hours helping him or her.

I began making some mistakes out of carelessness. Some out of boredom too, I believe. The work felt rote. I hungered to do something else. I even sensed that it was time to leave. I looked at new positions that sounded more energizing in other organizations. I came remarkably close to accepting one. But I found I didn't have the courage to leave, seduced as I was by the salary, the social standing, and the prestige of holding such a prominent position. My head and ego didn't want me to step away from all that—even if my heart and soul did.

So I stayed. And paid a price.

For the three final years I worked there, I woke up almost every morning hating to go to work that once enlivened me. I hated the rush-hour traffic. I hated the office I had once loved. Some people there began to irritate me, and I let it show, which was not professional or in keeping with my personal standards. That which had once given life had become unbearable—emotionally, professionally, personally, and spiritually.

Other things went wrong. And wronger. Until I had to leave. That was clear to me and to them. For their sake and mine. And so, despite my innate fear of leaving that which is secure, I did leave.

Life Lines

Relax your body, mind, and spirit.

Take two or three deep breaths.

Put the book down and think about the following slowly and gently.

Am I aware of indications that something has lost its liveliness for me? Or that it has ceased to be life-giving at all? What might those signs be?

As difficult as leaving was, after I did, life came back. Creativity did as well. That didn't make it any less of a scary time. A time of adventure that, at age sixty-one, I hadn't planned on. But, as you read in chapter 1, this adventure gave me the opportunity to practice beauty, truth, life, and love as I sought to discern my new place in this new time. And by paying attention to those four ideals, the right place for me appeared in God's good timing.

I was happy to be once again in a position where I could be more creative and less administrative than I had been. My former organization continues to grow and thrive, which makes me happy. My leaving was ultimately life-giving for them and me.

Do I wish I'd have read the life signs earlier? Indeed. No small pieces of anguish would have been avoided. But I am, at least in part, the man I am today from having gone through the anguish. A better man. That's because I learned from the pain of staying too long in a position that was no longer right for me.

I learned to choose life as well as how to recognize a bit easier when the life was gone and it was time for me to be gone as well.

Quaker spiritual director Patricia Loring once wrote:

The central issue is always, "Where is the Spirit leading you?" If God sets before us every day the choice of Life and Death and says, "Choose Life!" (Deut. 30:19–29), where is Life? Biblically, it is in love of and obedience to God; "staying close to the Root," as earlier Friends might have said. It may not always be gaiety, song and dance, or even snuggling babies; but neither will it be grim duty. It will be the place that touches the "quick"—an old word for where the life is in oneself: life answering Life. One of the traditional Quaker tests of the authenticity of a leading has been, "Is there Life in it?"

If we want to live the life that only we can live, we won't just ask, Will this bring life? as we begin a new ministry, relationship, committee assignment, project, or whatever. We need to take holy pauses and ask, Does this still bring life?

This is a question we need to ask often. When we can no longer answer, "Yes!" then it is time to consider whether it, whatever *it* is, has come to a close for us. A wavering yes might be a sign that it's time to consider moving on. No matter how difficult that moving on might be. If the liveliness is no longer there, then consider that this might be the Spirit's way of saying, "This is no longer yours to do. I have new work for you." If God is truly in something, it will continue to be invigorating. Rejuvenating.

Life Lines _____

Relax your body, mind, and spirit.

Take two or three deep breaths.

Put the book down and think about the following slowly and gently.

Do I take time to examine whether a thing that started out life-giving still is so? How do I know when something's time has come to a close?

Again, this isn't to say that because something is difficult, there's no life in it. Indeed, there may be all sorts of liveliness in those things that are difficult. My friend Christina Repoley had a vision for founding an organization in which young adults such as herself were empowered to discern and live into their gifts and callings. So, she set to work birthing Quaker Voluntary Service (QVS), where young adults commit eleven months to living at the intersection of transformational spirituality and activism.

The QVS fellows accepted into the program work full-time in professional positions at community-based organizations around the United States. They also live in a cooperative house and worship with, and are mentored by, local Quakers.

Founding and growing this movement was not easy. It was demanding work. But, as shown by the fruits of her labor, Christina was engaged in a life-giving endeavor. A lively vocation. For herself and for those who do a QVS year.

Christina was also wise because she kept asking Loring's question as QVS grew and thrived. When some of the life and liveliness in her position as founding director began to wane, she saw it was time to hand the reins over to new leadership. So she did. And she has moved on to other projects that give her life, and life abundantly.

Such experiences as Christina's show us that we need to change the big question from, What is the meaning of life? to, What gives my life meaning? You are the only one who can answer that. It might be your family. Your faith. Your job. What is it that gives your life deep and satisfying meaning? My guess is that your answer will be centered on something that has to do with what gives you a sense of purpose—a reason to be. Certainly, living a life of love of God and toward our fellow pilgrims leads to a life of purpose, meaning, and vigor.

If we live such a life, I believe we will inevitably encounter the meaning of life, though it probably won't be couched in philosophical linguistics. The abundant life entails intersecting our lives in love with one another and God. Doing so results in us living vigorously, infused with an aliveness that comes from inhabiting the life God created us to have.

Vivacity

The abundant life is more than just existing. Though that is obvious, I, at least, need to be reminded of it from time to time. The life God calls us to is meant to impart exuberance. Enthusiasm. Vivacity.

We all know people who embody vivacity. Their lives exude liveliness; whimsy and sprightliness.

When I think of someone whose vivaciousness springs from deep inside, Kelly Daugherty comes to mind. I met Kelly over thirty years ago when he was an office equipment salesman. I usually shy away from salespeople, as I find that many of them want to . . . well . . . sell me something. Which is not surprising. That's their job. I quickly discovered, though, that Kelly was someone I wanted to spend time with, even if he did sell me a photocopy machine.

That's because Kelly loves people. He likes selling, too, and believes in the products he sells. He finds genuine joy in meeting strangers and making them friends and then being able to help them with their needs.

I knew another fellow in the same company. I'll call him Not-Kelly. Not-Kelly always seemed to be only concerned about making a sale. Racking up numbers. Moving product. I found him smooth, cold, and unappealing. Now, I'm sure he's a nice person. He's good at his job. He's a highly successful salesman.

But Kelly . . . Kelly projects a positive delight in living. His meeting people gives him life. His helping people feeds his spirit. He's a man of deep faith, and I think he has aligned his genuine caring for people and his desire to do the life-giving work God created him to do into a fulfilling vocation.

I know he genuinely cares for his clients because when I was one of them, I found myself leaving a job and a marriage. Kelly would check on me just to see how I was doing. Then he offered me a job. He did it because, wrongly it turned out, he thought I'd be a good photocopier salesperson. But he did it mostly because he saw my need for a job and he could provide that. Yes, he hoped I'd love sales as much as him. I didn't. I'm an introvert, and the thought of going out to meet strangers and sell them office equipment terrified me. I was lousy at it.

But, because of Kelly's care for me, I moved to a new town to work for him. In that town I made lifelong friends and found a church family that cared for me. All because of a photocopier salesman who loved life, loved people, and lived God's abundant life.

Life Lines ─────────────────────────

Relax your body, mind, and spirit.

Take two or three deep breaths.

Put the book down and think about the following slowly and gently.

Who do I know that I'd describe as vivacious? What characteristics of that person that come from deep in her or his soul manifest themselves in such verve?

My friend Beth Collea is another one of those people for me. She is one of the most consistently enthusiastic people I've ever met. It's life-giving to be around her. On long car rides, when we traveled in ministry throughout New England, I always felt energized by her clear thinking and the way she saw possibilities instead of problems. Meals and other conversations with her and her husband, Jeremiah, are full of life. She draws others full of life to her and into her conversations and projects.

One of Beth's favorite words is *zesty*. When she comes across an idea or project that speaks to her, she often describes it as zesty. When she leads a presentation, no matter how serious the topic, participants come away feeling inspired and ready to get to work. That's because she is zesty and makes others want to be as well.

I want to be clear that Beth's is no shallow vivacity. No, her zest is rooted in a deep spiritual life. We all know people who seem vivacious but who are actually vacuous. They sort of exemplify Gertrude Stein's famous quote about Oakland, California, that "there's no there there." With Beth, there's a lot of there there.

Her deep life of the spirit renews and refreshes her—and those she works with. She makes spiritual vivacity something to aspire to. Beth's vivacity springs from her learning (whether she had ever read them or not) the truth of the words of William Stanley Braithwaite's poem:

To feed my soul with beauty till I die;
To give my hands a pleasant task to do;
To keep my heart forever filled anew
With dreams and wonders which the days supply;
To love all conscious living, and thereby
Respect the brute who renders up its due,
And know the world as planned is good and true—
And thus—because there chanced to be an I!

This is my life since things are as they are:
One half akin to flowers and the grass:
The rest a law unto the changeless star.
And I believe when I shall come to pass
Within the Door His hand shall hold ajar
I'll leave no echoing whisper of Alas!

Beth recognizes the precious everyday things of the life God has blessed her with. The birds at Jeremiah's backyard feeders. The joy of a good meal and conversation well shared. The wonderful discovery of a new idea. Her extended family. She sees the zest in everyday life and embraces it. And in so doing she is open to seeing the zest in all things big or small.

Life Lines ─────────────────────────────

Relax your body, mind, and spirit.

Take two or three deep breaths.

Put the book down and think about the following slowly and gently.

*How often do the things in my daily life add zest to my life? Are there
actions I could take or attitudes I might need to change to make such relish
possible?*

The Life-Giving Holy Ordinary

Beth's seeing life as she lives her daily life reminds me that if I want
to live abundantly and with vivacity, vim, and vigor, I too need to see
the holy in the ordinary life that makes up my days. I need to live in
wonder and awe in the place that I am. That way God can continue to
amaze and amuse and enliven me.

As a child, I went to an elementary school named for the great
naturalist John Burroughs. It was not until I was much older, though,
that I read these words of his:

The most precious things of life are near at hand, without money
and without price. Each of you has the whole wealth of the universe
at your very door. . . . The great globe swings around to him like a
revolving showcase; the change of the seasons is like the passage
of strange and new countries; the zones of the earth, with all their
beauties and marvels, pass one's door and linger long in the passing.

These precious things without money and without price are life-giving. They are blessings. When we read Scripture, we learn that one who understands that he or she is blessed has a rich and abundant life. As we dive into the biblical meanings of the words "rich" and "abundant," we find that they have to do with quality of life and its relationships—especially the relationship we have with God.

We sometimes forget that the "ordinary" relationships enliven us when we recognize them for the blessings they are. Kids, even the youngest of them, seem to have a better grasp of that than we adults do.

When I was a pastor at a Quaker meeting in Muncie, Indiana, I met every Thursday with the preschoolers attending our school. One Thursday before Thanksgiving, I asked them if they knew what holiday was coming up. I thought they would say Christmas since television commercials had begun suggesting gifts and the local mall was brimming with decorations. There was no hesitation, however, as together they shouted out "Thanksgiving."

That was a nice surprise.

Then I asked them if they knew what Thanksgiving was about.

"It's about giving thanks," they said. "Thanks to God for the stuff we have." Again, I was pleased—both with their innate sense of a time for giving thanks and with the good job their teachers had done in educating them about this holiday. Next, I asked what they were thankful for. I was ready for a list of favorite toys and games. Again, I was surprised.

"My family."

"My mommy."

"My daddy."

"My house."

"My friends."

"My sister."

"My dog."

"I have a dog," added another one.

"Not me, I have a cat," chimed another kid.

Not one of those kids first thought thankfulness had anything to do with possessions. They all had to do with relationships and home.

I think we would do well to remember how blessed we are with these things without money and without price. The kids were grateful for the blessings of simple pleasures. The simple things John Burroughs extolled. Maybe they really aren't so simple after all.

Not if we allow them to give us life, that is.

We can find these small things life-giving regardless of our age or station in life. And when we find them as such, we can extend them as life-giving gifts to others. We simply need to offer them up, in all their ordinariness, to God's touch with the prayer that they will be a blessing to those we meet. We need to know that the little acts of random kindness and love that we share with our fellow travelers on life's highway enliven them as well as us. Easing the way for one another is one of the most life-giving things we can do. As Iris DeMent sings,

> But I gave joy to my mother
> And I made my lover smile.
> And I can give comfort to my friends when they're hurting.
> I can make it seem better, I can make it seem better
> I can make it seem better for awhile.

The things she sings of are the things that give our lives value. Purpose. Gusto. We find our calling in bringing people joy, making the ones we love smile, and giving comfort to our friends and making it seem better for a while.

Whichever of those we are called to, it will be enough. It will bring life—and life in all its fulfillment and glory.

Life Lines

Relax your body, mind, and spirit.

Take two or three deep breaths.

Put the book down and think about the following slowly and gently.

What simple things that I experience daily give me life? Why is it such things feed my spirit?

"Oh, the good life, full of fun, seems to be the ideal," sang Tony Bennett. Well, his good life full of fun may be the ideal of many, but it does not provide the soulful satisfaction of the abundant life Jesus says he came to bring. When we align our daily existence with the life-giving things that God created us to have, we find that we have lives that are more than full of fun. Our days, good and bad, easy or rough, will be quickened by the presence of the Spirit with us. The things we do will give us energy instead of draining us. Our relationships, including our one with the God who loves us more than we can imagine, will renew us. We will be led from life to more life, one of continual growth and adventures big and small.

Our life-giving God offers us the opportunity to be so engaged in being fully alive that at the end of our day or week or whenever, we might find ourselves sitting by the light of the fire of our life, watching the sparks fly, and say with every fiber of our being, "This is living!"

CHAPTER 5
Love—Being Directed by Heart

The greatest of these is love.
—1 CORINTHIANS 13:13

The whole worth of a kind deed lies in the love that inspires it.
—THE TALMUD

"Brent, you're a good writer," said my friend and editor Lil Copan. I smiled. Then she followed up with, "Would you like to be a great one?"

Wow, what a question. There was no other way to answer except, "Yes!" I mean, I was pretty comfortable with good. I was technically sound. I could produce articles and books to publishers' and editors' expectations. I had done that for years. I turned out fine pieces of writing that people found helpful and/or entertaining.

But Lil recognized something was missing. That was my heart. Most of my writing came from my head. Yes, I cared about the things I wrote about, but I stayed largely hidden emotionally. I rarely revealed much of myself. "You almost let the reader get to know you," she continued, "and then you pull back and play it safe. Write more boldly, more openly. More from the heart."

That was advice I needed. I followed it and found my writing became more satisfying for me and certainly for the reader, judging by comments I receive.

What's that got to do with love? Just this. While we all love, we want to be more than just good lovers—our heads and our emotions urge us to hold back. To play it safe. Yet our hearts tell us to be bold and open. We all have many lessons to learn about loving. As Over the Rhine sings,

> We're all still beginners
> We're all late bloomers
> When it comes to love

Perhaps that's why Saint Paul, in the twelfth chapter of 1 Corinthians, after talking about the various gifts God has given us, ends by saying that we should desire God's greater gifts and concludes, "I will show you the most excellent way." He then takes us into one of the best-known chapters of the Bible—the Love Chapter, as it is known by many—and thereby shows why love is the most excellent way.

It is the most excellent way in part because learning to live in love warms our lives as we discover how to rest more fully into God's deep love for us. God is a being of radiant love who reaches out to us. God also knows that we need to see that love in action too. Besides coming clothed in human flesh in Jesus to demonstrate the depth of that love more fully, God shows it every day through the kindness of our fellow travelers and the unexpected little graces that come into our lives in the midst of the various mists we may find ourselves fumbling through. There are all around us people of faith who—when we are in the middle of darkness, doubt, despair, joy, happiness, and light—say to us on God's behalf, "I love you. I love you. I love you. I love you."

And thereby they point us to the most excellent way.

Children of a God of Radiant Love

We know that God is love, but we tend to forget how overwhelming that love is. The second chapter of Luke, which we hear a lot during the Christmas season, illustrates the radiance of God's love in a way that few other biblical passages do. In this piece of Scripture, Luke shows us this radiance in action.

Think of it! What Luke describes is no passive expression of emotion. This is God entering into relationship with us in a way that is almost incomprehensible. If we weren't so familiar with the story, it would seem unbelievable to us. God steps into human life and history clothed in the same flesh that we are. In doing so, divine love becomes more than something about which we're told—we see it in the reality of Jesus's daily life and interactions with those around him. The stories show us God's love for all his children as Jesus sups with sinners, heals the sick, feeds the hungry, makes the blind (and not just the physically blind) see again. Tax collectors, seeking Pharisees, adulteresses, spiritual outcasts, and more are welcomed by this "Firstborn of Mary, provocative preacher, itinerant teacher, outsider's choice."

The person of Jesus reveals that the One who is in and over all cares for us—not just collectively, but individually. It shows that God is not like Linus Van Pelt of *Peanuts*, who declares, "I love mankind—it's people I can't stand." No, God loves us personally, individually, and deeply with what the early Quaker George Fox called "the infinite love of God."

Love Letters

Relax your body, mind, and spirit.

Take two or three deep breaths.

Put the book down and think about the following slowly and gently.

When is a time in my life that I have felt the infinite, wonderful, all-embracing love of God? How did I know that was from God?

This deep, deep love is something we often are unable to grasp. It is also hard for us to imagine that God pursues us because of that love. Christine Kelly's poem "Unrequited Lover" helps me bring into focus the reality of God as the great lover of my soul:

Every day,
I walk by your house and bring you flowers . . .
sunsets, butterflies, the Big Dipper.

I hide,
just around the corner, planning
to catch your smile of surprise, and then
I AM! would rush right out
and grab you in my arms
and we'd laugh and talk and find
delight
in each other.

But I piped for you and you did not dance.
I wailed and you did not mourn.
Yet all I ever wanted was to give you
my Kingdom.

Every day,
I walk by your house
and bring you flowers. . . .

That's the kind of love God has for us. And so, in the same way I have finally learned to relax into the love those closest to me have for me, I also need to learn to relax in the steadfast love of God. That is a love that surrounds and constantly watches over us. When we are awake. When we're asleep. When we rejoice. When we mourn.

Love Letters

Relax your body, mind, and spirit.

Take two or three deep breaths.

Put the book down and think about the following slowly and gently.

What would it feel like to relax in the deep love of God? How would that feel in my brain? In my heart? In my body?

God only wants to love us. I think Robert Penn Warren's poem "Interjection #6: What You Sometimes Feel On Your Face at Night," with its "perhaps" in the last line, eloquently expresses our human amazement at such a divine miracle as that kind of love.

As I learn to relax in God's love for me, though, I also need to remember that a way I can reciprocate that love is to seek where I may serve. When I live with humility and patience in service to others, I share, in small ways, the love of God on earth. When we children of our loving God collectively do that, then we show the world what it means to be loved—and to love.

I want to live that most excellent way. I want to feel divine love enveloping me. I want to bask in that radiant love and thereby be taught how to love. Then I will be better prepared to say on God's behalf to those I meet, "I love you. I love you. I love you. I love you."

What Does Love Look Like?

I live out in the country. Ploughshares is too far from the city to pick up antenna signals, no cable company wants to invest in running lines to the few houses on our rural road, and the internet service is so slow that a show broadcast in Indianapolis is in reruns by the time it streams on my iPad. Okay, that latter is a bit of an exaggeration. Still, if I want to watch television, I have to subscribe to a satellite television service. The package I have comes with 170 channels. That's about 125 more than I need, but it's the only one that has the old-movie and sports channels I want to watch.

That means there are lots of channels I'd love to drop. Especially those that show sappily sentimental cinema. Bleh. Those movies make me cringe. Mostly because the love they portray looks very little like my experience of what love really looks like. Love rarely looks like quaint cottages set in the English countryside, or long, desire-filled gazes over glasses of fine wine and exquisitely prepared meals, or carefree convertible cruises along the roads outside Moustiers-Sainte-Marie in southern France, with the lovers' hair perfectly coiffed, their skin unblemished, the conversation scintillating with just the right words said.

Those all sound good to me. Especially having my hair perfectly coiffed—which would mean that I still had hair! However, most of us learn what love looks like in the midst of daily life. While it might be easy to love that handsome, charming, wealthy man pouring you a flute of fine champagne as you lounge on his yacht anchored off the Grecian coast, chances are you more regularly find yourself sitting across the breakfast table with a fellow needing his hair combed and a good shave who leaves the toilet seat up and his dirty clothes in a heap outside the bathroom shower.

Love Letters _____

Relax your body, mind, and spirit.

Take two or three deep breaths.

Put the book down and think about the following slowly and gently.

How would I describe what love looks like? How do I know love when I see it?

The fact that sentimental television movies falsely portray love makes Saint Paul's description of love in 1 Corinthians 13 so important. It shows us what love should look like as we live our lives with those we love. Despite the heaps of dirty clothes and tousled hair. Love, he says,
   is patient,
   is kind,
   is not envious,
   does not boast,
   isn't proud,
   doesn't dishonor others,
   is not self-seeking,
   is not easily angered,
   keeps no record of wrongs,
   does not delight in evil,
   rejoices with the truth,
   protects,
   always trusts,
   always hopes,
   always perseveres,
   and never fails.

That's some list. It's a list that looks nothing like the love on those television movies that I dislike. Yet, despite the lack of mentioning sunlit meadows alive with birdsong and the longing gazes of a lover, each of the above describes the kind of love we long to experience. A love that is patient, kind, trusting, hopeful, protective, and persevering. All of them coming from a lover who isn't envious or boastful, self-seeking or easily angered, and doesn't keep a record of wrongs.

When we find such a love and lover, our hearts thrill. We feel complete and cared for. We breathe deeply and live easily. Our striving ceases and we soak up the light of that love. We are renewed. Life blossoms.

Those words also should remind us that that's the kind of lovers we should be. Or at least I should be. I'm not always patient or kind. Sometimes I do keep a record of wrongs—no matter how minor.

Love Letters

Relax your body, mind, and spirit.

Take two or three deep breaths.

Put the book down and think about the following slowly and gently.

As I look over the list from 1 Corinthians 13, which ones are the hardest for me to put into practice? Why might that be? What holds me back?

I am an imperfect lover. As are we all this side of eternity. But sometimes we get it just enough right that it brings joy, happiness, and peace to those we love. And for a time, it is enough. It is just right.

While our love is imperfect (though still wonderful!), we are offered an experience of perfect love. That's the love God shows us. We are wooed by the Great Lover of our souls, who hopes to win us with the winsomeness of that love.

Still that often feels like an abstract sort of love. A concept; not so much something we feel. So I invite you to develop some very clear images of love for you. The following exercise is meant to help you do just that. I'd like you to be as concrete as possible as you walk through this exercise—to move from abstract concepts to fully fleshed examples that fit your experience. You do that by completing the following phrases:

Love looks visually like . . .
Love tastes like . . .
Love sounds like . . .
Love smells like . . .
Love feels tactilely like . . .

Next, let's change it up a bit:

God's love looks visually like . . .
God's love tastes like . . .
God's love sounds like . . .
God's love smells like. . .
God's love feels tactilely like . . .

While the above exercise might appear slightly silly, I find it helpful as I try to think concretely about what love is. Including where love is in the things I feel God wants me to do. If love is not present in the things I think God might want me to do, then I probably shouldn't do them because I'd be doing them from some less-than-pure motive.

I often need help remembering to look for the signs of love. I find I can do that by thinking concretely about my physical indicators of love—outside, "real" factors rather than just my "heady" thoughts of love. Knowing those indicators is important because as Swiss theologian and Catholic priest Hans Urs von Balthasar said, "Once a person learns to read the signs of love and thus to believe it, love leads him into the open field wherein he himself can love."

Reading the signs and living out of, and through, the power of love ensures that we undertake our souls' work in goodness and with the right attitudes. Paying attention to the signs of love helps God's love and light shine in and through us so that we might truly do the work that is ours to do in the transformative power of divine love. Saint Augustine said that love gives us "the hands to help others. It has the feet to hasten to the poor and needy. It has eyes to see misery and want. It has the ears to hear the sighs and sorrows of men. That is what love looks like." Such a love is a long way from what I see on those television movies.

Such love also warms our lives as we live more fully into God's deep love for us. The God of love calls us to be people of love. As we grow in God's love we become active signs of that love in the world and to the people around us.

Love Doesn't Mean Easy

Falling in love is easy. I used to do it all the time when I was a teenager. Every day, in fact. That's because every day I encountered young women new to me. I fell in love with them because of their beauty, their charm, their grace, and the fact that they had not rejected me yet.

Falling in love is easy. But loving day to day is harder. Putting into action the things that Saint Paul listed, that is. I can feel emotional and loving without necessarily doing anything about it. The question is not, Do I love? but rather, If I I love, what am I going to do about it? How do I express it? How do I act?

I once heard someone say that love is not a feeling, but rather it is a lifelong series of actions. When I heard it, I questioned the truth of that statement. I was all for love so long as it meant going on dates, buying cards and flowers, and professing love to my latest sweetheart. That was easy.

I've since learned that loving beyond fleeting emotion and putting love into play in works of kindness, compassion, helpfulness, and more is often difficult. Such loving takes a lifetime of practice. Especially if we are to love people other than just those whom we are in love with.

But for now, let's look at loving one person. "Love is difficult," said Rainer Maria Rilke.

> For one human being to love another human being: that is perhaps the most difficult task that has been entrusted to us, the ultimate task, the final test and proof, the work for which all other work is merely preparation.

In my life, I think of that difficult task as it relates to the first person I loved. Jo Ann Shields Bill. My mother. Hers was the first face (after Dr. George Clouse) that I saw after entering this world. My love as an infant and toddler was based on what she did for me; how she cared for me. Later it grew deeper and was more reciprocal. Throughout our lives together, it was tested (especially during my teenage years!) and grew. With every passing year, I learned to love her more deeply and show it better through my actions. This lifelong lesson in love culminated in my sitting on her bed, stroking her hair as I helped birth her into the Great Mystery beyond this life in the same way she birthed me into this life. Different pains, but still painful, despite great love.

Still, learning to love Mom as fully as I wished in actions and not just words was comparatively easy compared to learning to love others. Especially those others with whom I have no deep or lasting connection. And yet Jesus said the second great commandment was "Love your neighbor as yourself." Throughout his teaching he revealed that everyone else on this planet was my neighbor and should therefore be loved by me.

No exceptions.

Love Letters

Relax your body, mind, and spirit.

Take two or three deep breaths.

Put the book down and think about the following slowly and gently.

Do I agree with Rilke that loving another human being is the most difficult task we're given in this life? What does it mean for me to truly love another person?

Loving the way Jesus says I should is really difficult. At least in reality. In the abstract, I can say I love everybody. But when I have to put love into action in real life, I have to admit there are some people I don't want to love. I don't like them—their actions, their attitudes, their political views, the way they treat those I love, the way they treat the oppressed and downtrodden, the way they act toward *me*.

In 1693, William Penn said, "Love is the hardest lesson in Christianity; but, for that reason, it should be most our care to learn it." Those words are as true today as they were almost 350 years ago. At least I find them so. And so, if I am to love as I am loved, and want to be known as a Christ-one, then I must stick to learning that hardest lesson.

But how can I learn to love those who are hard to love?

First, I need to remember that they are as loved by God as I am. I get that intellectually. But emotionally I'm more like Vizzini in *The Princess Bride*—"Inconceivable!" There is no way that God could love that (insert the adjectives that best describe the person I dislike the most here) person as much as God loves me.

But wait. God loves me? And how (insert the adjectives that best describe the person I dislike the most here) am I?

Sigh.

So, okay, first I need to love those people who are hard to love, or even like, because God loves them.

Second, I need to treat them as if I loved them. Whether I like them or not. In the case of one particularly irascible old man I found difficult, it meant seeing him through the eyes of someone who really did love him. When I did that, it helped me see the good, not just the irritating, in the old gent. Which meant I could mow his grass and stack his wood the way he wanted—which was not necessarily the way I would have done either of those tasks.

Third, I have to accept that my love may not be returned. Just because I love doesn't mean my love will be reciprocated. I need to abandon any expectation that it will.

To love as Christ loves me means I cannot see love as a transaction. Of course, I am not the lover that Christ is, so this lesson is especially difficult. I expect that if I love in my actions, then that love should be returned . . . or at the very least acknowledged. Moving beyond that expectation is not easy.

A fourth lesson in love is one that I learned from Jessica Powers, one of my favorite poets. In her poem "To Live with the Spirit," she writes, "To live with the Spirit of God is to be a listener," and "To live with the Spirit of God is to be a lover."

Listening is one of the keys to loving. As I think about that and when it's occurred in my own life, I find that it is true. When I truly listen, I can more easily love—even those I find hard to love.

That's because godly listening is an act of hospitality. An act of vulnerability. An act of laying aside my needs and myself in order to be open to the other. Love can grow when I create a space for listening and dialogue with others whose way led them to a place that I would not go. For me that often starts by asking them to tell me their story—

whatever that story is that I find as the sticking place in my ability to love them. It might be how they feel about faith. Social issues. Politics. And so on. Especially if the other is a person who professes faith, even when I can't see how someone who professes faith could believe or behave that way. I have to remember that they probably can't see my profession as real either. Regardless, my ability to love them can grow from being given a glimpse of their spiritual journey. I often have gained fresh insights I wouldn't have received without such an opportunity to hear about their life with God.

The only rule to this deep listening as a way of learning "the hardest lesson in Christianity" is, like our parents used to tell us, to "play nice." I've slowly learned not to argue or try to refute someone else's position. Rather I use such opportunities as ones of genuine curiosity and interest in how God is working (whether they realize it or not) in other people's lives. In other words, as much as possible, I listen for the following:

beauty
caring
faith
gentleness
goodness
joy
long-suffering
love
meekness
peace
persistence
rightness

In what places do they mirror my own? And where there's dissonance, I ask why in a way that searches my own soul.

As I listen that way (and I admit I don't do it often enough), I find myself being opened to love. Often that love begins as a small gleam of respect and understanding for the annoying other. A glimpse of their humanity and hopes and dreams. Listening to another with my spiritual ears wide open leads me closer to love—and God.

Love Letters ─────────────────────────

Relax your body, mind, and spirit.

Take two or three deep breaths.

Put the book down and think about the following slowly and gently.

What lessons about how to be loving have I learned throughout my life? How do I put them into practice in loving daily?

A final lesson I've learned—which is in some ways the hardest—is that if I truly love, then I don't need to meddle in that which is not my business. Instead, I need to be open and tender and let that which is not mine to worry about go. Jesus said, "Love your enemies, do good to them, and lend to them without expecting to get anything back."

I would rephrase that slightly to read, "Brent, love those you find difficult, do good to them, and love on them without expecting to get anything back"

When I do that, I can present the person, in love, to God and leave them there in the eternal, divine Love.

Love, the Vital Piece

"All you need is love," sang the Beatles. Well, it may not be all we need, but it is certainly vital. Especially, that is, if we want to discern and do the divine will for our lives. Love should be the root of all our actions. Likewise, love reveals what is ours to do. Thérèse of Lisieux had discovered that and wrote,

> Love gave me the key to my vocation. I realized that if the church was a body made up of different members, she would not be without the greatest and most essential of them all. I realized that love includes all vocations, that love is all things, and that, because it is eternal, it embraces every time and place. Swept by an ecstatic joy, I cried, "At last I have found my vocation. My vocation is love! I have found my place. I will be love. So I shall be everything and so my dreams will be fulfilled!"

Her quotation illustrates perfectly why the ultimate purpose of desiring to do the divine will should not be out of some sense of duty or "ought," but because it is that in which we will find our ultimate fulfillment as individuals and people of faith. Doing the divine will, if it starts aright, leads us from love into more love. In fact, as Thérèse's statement reveals, we move from being loving to being love. "I will be love." What a glorious thought. I won't just be doing love, but I will actually become love. Love becomes the vocation of our lives. When we grow into that reality, we will do what we love and we will love what we do.

Love Letters ───────────────

Relax your body, mind, and spirit.

Take two or three deep breaths.

Put the book down and think about the following slowly and gently.

Can I say with Thérèse that love has given me my vocation.
  Why or why not?

If we want to do what we love and we love what we do, we first need to know what love is. We need to come to a comprehension of its eternal, divine nature. The Quaker mystic Isaac Penington helps us gain that understanding when he answers his own question, "What is love?" by saying,

What shall I say of it, or how shall I in words express its nature? It is the sweetness of life; it is the sweet, tender, melting nature of God, flowing up through his seed of life into the creature, and of all things making the creature most like unto himself, both in nature and operation. It fulfils the law, it fulfils the gospel; it wraps up all in one, and brings forth all in the oneness. It excludes all evil out of the heart, it perfects all good in the heart. A touch of love doth this in measure; perfect love doth this in fullness.

God's love, as we live into it, melts our hearts, burning way the dross of self-centeredness and leaving the gold of goodness. This is not an instantaneous refining process. It takes the slow work of God's grace-full love to accomplish. I know my own heart contains the dross of self-centeredness, for example. Yet, slowly, as I endeavor to walk in the way of this love, I find that I am able to put more and more of my selfish nature behind and live lovingly, trusting love to guide me.

When I rely on divine love to guide me, then I find that my motives are more rightly ordered. They align more closely to God's will for my life that it be more one of joy, peace, forbearance, kindness, goodness, faithfulness, gentleness, and self-control and less one of should, ought, duty, condescension, and other less noble things. That's something saints through the ages have learned and practiced. John Woolman, an eighteenth-century Friend, felt led, in dangerous times, to travel to the then frontier of western Pennsylvania to meet with Native Americans there. One night on his journey, he reflected on why he felt called to do such a thing and concluded that "love was the first motion."

Not duty.

Not because he had great wisdom to share with these people that many of his contemporaries thought of as savages. No, because love moved him to do so.

That love informed his reason for going. As he writes, he desired

to spend some time with the Indians, that I might feel and understand their life and the spirit they live in, if haply I might receive some instruction from them, or they might be in any degree helped forward by my following the leadings of truth among them.

Love invited him to understand these first peoples of America and the nature of their spirit. Love helped him see that he might actually learn from them. Then, after those, he saw that they might be helped by his following that first motion of love to spend time among them. Not by anything he might do—worthy as it might be. But rather because any good work he did arose from love.

I saw that in action shortly after we built our house. Our home is on a ridge, tucked back against a woods. At that time five acres of former pasture sat directly in front of it. And we had another ten acres of former pasture ringed by woods in other places on our property.

When we were getting ready to build, I had seen that land primarily as money—an investment that could be sold when I retired and would give us a good income in the golden years. But after living in the house for a year and tramping around the old pastures and following deer and other animal tracks through them and the woods and along the creek, something unexpected happened. I began to fall in love with the land. The pastures' gentle risings and fallings. The coolness of wading in the creek on a sweltering day. The various trees and the fruits and nuts they bore.

So, I began reconsidering what I wanted to do with the land we then had. I did know I didn't want to keep it mowed. Having that large of an expanse of lawn seemed a terrible waste of my time and the resources it would take to keep it looking nice. I thought of all the fuel and the pollution caused by burning that fuel. So we met with various conservation people. Together we developed a plan to put in eight acres of woods in a lower pasture, along with eight acres of prairie and one acre of various fruit-bearing trees and berry bushes to encourage the reestablishment of wildlife in the pasture in front of our house.

We hired a forester to plant the lower eight acres. That involved getting 7,500 tree seedlings into the ground. The forester had a crew and the equipment needed to do it efficiently and in such a way we could keep the weeds from choking out the seedlings before they had a chance to take good root and grow.

Likewise, a local conservation group agreed to seed the prairie for a small donation. But Nancy decided that we should plant the four hundred trees and bushes that would grow as a buffer in the one acre between our yard and the prairie ourselves. She did not want them in orderly, evenly spaced rows as the machine planted trees in the lower field would be.

Four hundred trees are a lot of trees. Even if they are seedlings. Even if they supposedly require just a slit in the ground, slipping them in, and stamping the ground back into place. Fortunately, we have a large family and they all love Nancy. The call went out for a tree-planting party. We picked a date. We ordered the trees. The big day came—along with siblings, children, parents, grandchildren, nieces and nephews, the trees—and a downpour!

At the designated time, we donned raincoats, windbreakers, and hastily purchased one-size-fits-all ponchos, and headed out. I opened the first packet of trees and saw that the supposed "slit, slip, and stamp" method would not work. The trees were one to two feet tall with roots that extended two to three feet. We'd have to dig holes for each one. So, some of us started digging holes, others planted, and Nancy directed where various species should go—Kentucky coffee tree here, pawpaw there, blackberry bushes along the perimeter. All in the pouring rain.

Two hours later, we had planted all four hundred—along with some extras the Indiana Department of Natural Resources had thrown in. Family and friends stood there dripping, filthy, and smiling in wet grass and circles of mud. They had come not because of a deep love of conservation, or duty, or because a job needed doing. They came and worked in that rain because of one thing. Love. Love for their mother, sister, daughter-in-law, aunt, grandmother (and hopefully at least a little for me).

The work in the rain and mud followed easily and without grumbling—except for the good-natured kind. Especially when the sun broke through the clouds fifteen minutes after we planted the last tree. When I think of that day, and the love shown, my heart is warmed and tears of joy fill the corners of my eyes.

Love Letters

Relax your body, mind, and spirit.

Take two or three deep breaths.

Put the book down and think about the following slowly and gently.

When have I seen love in action? How did I know that love was the motivating force?

Love, the First Motion

Certainly a life filled with love and lived in love makes for a more abundant life. It is difficult to feel a lack of abundance when enveloped in love. Yet abundance only fully comes when we make it, as John Woolman said, the first motion.

His words have stuck in my soul since I first read them years ago. They sparked my imagination and fired my heart. When I read them, I wondered what it would be like to really let love be the guiding principle of all that I was to say—and do!

I've often heard Saint Augustine quoted as having said, "Love God and do what you please." I'm not certain he said those actual words, but I have often wondered what it would be like to "Love God and do what I *loved*." Would that be too centered in my own affections? Or could it be that the seed of divine love that God has placed in my heart might actually lead me aright? In the same way it did Woolman on his trip to visit the Native Americans?

I wrote earlier about all the missionary meetings I went to as a kid and how much I didn't want to be a missionary. I had the innate sense that my becoming a missionary was not true to my life. I still feel that. And I understand, when I think about love being the first motion, that one major reason my being a missionary wouldn't be true to my life is that I would not be doing so out of love. I wouldn't love being a missionary. I wouldn't love raising funds to support my work. I wouldn't love whatever place I would be sent. But most of all I wouldn't be doing it because I loved the people.

Yes, I loved them in the abstract. After all, Jesus told me I had to. But it was the love of the ennobled for the benighted. So if I became a missionary, I'd be going to those poor people only because they needed my superior understandings of life, the Bible, the true Christian way, God, Jesus, the Holy Spirit, and, perhaps most of all, the way they should live. I would be going out of a sense of duty, picking up "the white man's burden" as Rudyard Kipling called it in his paean to Christian America's imperialist vision. I wouldn't be doing it because I genuinely cared for them as individuals and beloved children of God who had more to teach me than I could ever hope to teach them. I would be the very worst of the worst missionaries because I had not love.

It took me years to understand that and see the lack of love in my heart. And to learn to leave good and helpful mission work to those for whom love was truly the first motion. As I learned that, I also saw the truth behind William Penn's statement that "love is the hardest lesson in Christianity." It certainly was for me. And so, as Penn said, I had to be careful to learn it. Learning it meant learning to listen for the motions of love in my life, including the things I should do with and in my life.

Love Letters

Relax your body, mind, and spirit.

Take two or three deep breaths.

Put the book down and think about the following slowly and gently.

Have I felt motions of love in my life, urging me to do something? What clues did I have that they came from love and not something else?

If, as I believe, life calls to life, then so too does love call to love. If we love God and then endeavor to do what we love, we find ourselves moving deeper into lives that we love. Lives that are more beautiful, true, and filled with life.

Living love that way means that we need to learn to trust the hearts and souls that God gave us. Doing so moves us from a ledger-sheet sort of thinking (Column 1: God Wants; Column 2: I Want), being too often governed by our head, to a way of life that integrates our whole selves into the divine will. Trusting our hearts to be wise and divinely led takes us into more soul-satisfying, and therefore abundant, lives.

Now I am not speaking here of giving ourselves over to hedonistic, narcissistic whims or urges. No. I am talking about living in divine love that radiates from our human hearts—from the seed planted in us that calls us toward that love which is eternal and life-giving. That love, says Thomas à Kempis,

> flies, runs, leaps for joy; it is free and unrestrained, resting in One who is highest above all things, from whom every good flows and proceeds. Love does not regard the gifts, but turns to the Giver of all good gifts. Love knows no limits, but ardently transcends all bounds. Love feels no burden, takes no account of toil, attempts things beyond its strength; love sees nothing as impossible, for it feels able to achieve all things. Love therefore does great things; it is strange and effective; while he who lacks love faints and fails.

What a glorious picture of what living with love as the first motion can be like in our vocations, our relationships, our committee work, our service to others. Yes, when you read it there are obvious parallels to Saint Paul's chapter on love, but à Kempis adds an exuberance that is inviting.

When given an opportunity, no matter what that opportunity is, in our lives, we need to ask if any urge to say yes to it comes from love—or something else. Does it

> make my spirit soar?
> feel unlike a burden?
> make my heart glad?
> renew my soul?
> give me hope?
> help me become more Christlike?
> change me in good ways?
> invite me to do something close to the heart of God?

Is it

sweet or bitter?
joyful or sorrowful?
tender or hardened?
free or restrained?
limitless or limited?
life-giving or life-draining?

If our joyful yes comes from the positive things above, then we can move forward with assurance that we are saying yes from love. We are saying yes from our hearts and the heart of God.

Love Letters

Relax your body, mind, and spirit.

Take two or three deep breaths.

Put the book down and think about the following slowly and gently.

Is there anything that holds me back from saying yes to love moving in and through me?

The love in the four ideals of beauty, truth, life, and love is no drudgery type of love. No! The love God wills for us consists of living a life of love that flies, leaps, and is free. It frees us to live fully into the people God created us to be and to do the things God meant for us to do.

From that kind of life of love, every good—for us and those we encounter—will flow. To the benefit of our souls. And to the glory of God.

CHAPTER 6

Weaving Beauty, Truth, Life, and Love into the Tapestry of Life

*Love is the fruit of beauty. When you see a beautiful tree,
you fall in love—ah, beautiful flowers, the bluebells,
the primroses! Beauty enters the heart and creates love.
That is why in the world today we lack love, because there is less
and less beauty in our everyday lives.*
—SATISH KUMAR

Beauty, truth, life, and love are centered on the very essence of the life God desires for us to live. I said that in the opening chapter. I say it again here because I think it's crucial for us to remember that if we really want to live the abundant life. When we seek beauty, truth, life, and love in all we are and do, then we do more than just exist; we grow and blossom into the people we were created to be. Then we find ourselves limned with a luminosity that comes from deep within us that lights our path and guides our way as we move through this world. The abundant life becomes more than just a concept. It becomes our reality.

Now before you think I'm painting too rosy a picture of the impact of beauty, truth, life, and love in our lives, let me assure you that I'm well aware that life is hard at times. The abundant life is not all joy and kitty pictures. Not every moment sparkles the way we'd like it to. Not this side of eternity, that is.

When I think of that, I think of Brother Lawrence doing dishes and repairing sandals in the priory of the Discalced Carmelites in Paris. Kitchen work and fixing stinking sandals hardly sounds like an abundant life. And yet, Brother Lawrence made it so because he practiced those things to the glory of God.

He found that the most effective way of living his life in and with God was by doing daily work out of love. He wisely believed—and that wisdom was passed on to us in the little book *The Practice of the Presence of God*—that every activity can unite us with God. Not just the sacred times. Not just the glorious times. But all times.

When I read *The Practice of the Presence of God*, as I have many times since high school, I find a man who had endured hardships and yet found an abundant life of beauty, truth, life, and love. Born to peasant parents, he became a soldier as a way to have regular meals and make a small amount of money. But it was the time of the Thirty Years' War. He fought against the Swedes, French, and Germans. He suffered greatly, and then he joined the Carmelites, deciding to sanctify his daily life and work by living a life of love of God.

"Ah, yes," you may say, "but he was a saint. One of those rare ones who can look beyond this veil of flesh into the world of spirit." Indeed, he was a saint. But not because he possessed something we do not. Rather because he chose to look for God in the holy ordinary of his life. The dishes. The sandals. The service to others. In them he found beauty. Truth. Life. Love.

Perhaps seventeenth-century France seems like a simpler time compared to ours. And he was safely ensconced in a monastery, while we are not. We are in the real modern world fraught with peril and business and busyness. Maybe that made it easier for Lawrence to practice these ideals.

Well, I doubt, could Lawrence visit us today, that he would find our times any more fraught than his own. Wars. Sickness. Famine. Certainly doing dishes and repairing sandals is no less drudgery than working in a cubicle or on an assembly line or in a fast-food restaurant. What made the difference between his finding an abundant life and our own lack of the same was that he learned early on to seek the four ideals in all he did. In his seeking, he found them. And the abundant life opened for him.

In my own life, even as I try to keep the ideals of beauty, truth, life, and love present at all times, doing so can become difficult. I experience periods of grief when I lose those dear to me. There are times when my chores feel like a grind. I get frustrated with the politics of hate and meanness that seem to surround me. I'm also a person who has struggled with depression a good bit of my adult life. Being hounded by the black dog, I call it.

At times such as those, it is hard to see my life as abundant. Especially if I think of the abundant life as perfect and easy. But such times have taught me that they come not because I lack faith. They have nothing to do with who I am as a spiritual person. Nothing to do, that is, in the sense that I experience them as a result of some sort of spiritual failing. As things that would go away if I only believed more. Behaved better. Read my Bible more intensely. Prayed with more passion. No. They are just part of my living in this life in this world in this time.

When I look, though, for beauty, truth, life, and love even in the midst of hard times, I can catch glimpses of their presence. When I'm grieving, for example, I remember with love the dear one who has passed and all the beauty and truth and life that flowed through them into me.

In other trying times, I often find those four ideals shining through the lives of my friends who come for a visit or who call or write at just the time I needed it.

I also cling to the words of Saint Paul when he says, "We know that in all things God works for the good of those who love him." I read that as meaning God fits all of our lives into a pattern that turns out for good. Perhaps some of the threads composing the pattern for the tapestry of our lives are short. Others are long. Some may even be broken. Certainly, Tristan Bernard, the French playwright, poet, and novelist, could well have thought a major thread of his and his wife's life tapestry was broken when they were arrested by the Gestapo during World War II. At that moment, before being imprisoned, however, he told his wife, "The time of fear is over. The time of hope has begun." The thread of fear was broken. The thread of hope began to be weaved into their tapestry.

Our time of fear, of living in lack and unhappiness, and moving toward hope and abundance, happens when we make beauty, truth, life, and love more than just some of the threads in the tapestry of our lives. We need to make them the warps.

A tapestry, you see, comprises two main components: the warp and the weft.

The weft threads are the ones we see when we look at a tapestry. They are the colored pieces that run horizontally and combine to form the completed picture a tapestry presents to the viewer. They can be long. They can be short. These threads don't run through the entire tapestry. That's why they're technically knowns as "discontinuous wefts." Each thread is knotted or tucked into place and then another is added. This process continues until the picture is formed.

However, each of these thousands of threads need something to anchor them. Those are the warp. The warp runs vertically. Warp thread is also heavier than weft threads, which is why they make good anchors for the tapestry.

If we use beauty, truth, life, and love as our warp threads, then everything that comes into our life—big or small, easy or difficult, happy or sad—is used as a weft to weave the amazing tapestry of our abundant life with God.

Another thing that is important about a tapestry is that, historically, when making a tapestry the weavers worked from the back, not the front. While they worked with a design, called a cartoon, many did so while looking at its reflection in a mirror as the cartoon hung on the wall. The weavers did not see the completed image until the last weft was tucked into the warp and the tapestry was turned over to be viewed as a whole.

So it is with our lives. Again, to quote Saint Paul, "For now we see only a reflection as in a mirror; then we shall see face to face. Now I know in part; then I shall know fully, even as I am fully known." While Paul was a tentmaker by trade, he may have known about tapestry construction. Some fragments of Grecian tapestries have been found that date to the third century BCE.

We weave the tapestry of our lives never seeing the entire finished product in our time here on earth. At best, we work from a cartoon looking in a mirror. Seeing a reflection. We set the warp of beauty, truth, life, and love. We weave the weft in part. The design we're working from will produce, with divine assistance, a beautiful picture of a life well-lived.

Full.

Rich.

Pleasing.

Abundant.

ACKNOWLEDGMENTS

My life has been graced with many people who taught me the value of living a life of beauty, truth, life, and love by doing so themselves. They are too many to mention. I tip my Quaker hat to them all, but most especially to my late parents, John and Jo Ann Bill.

I particularly want to recognize the Friends of Lake Erie Yearly Meeting. Their invitation to me to be their keynote speaker at their 2012 annual sessions gave me the impetus to clarify and put into words something I'd been wrestling with. This book truly is a result of that invitation.

The good people at Paraclete Press demonstrate beauty, truth, life, and love in the care and workmanship they put into each book—from designing beautiful covers to interior design and more. I appreciate these folks more than I can adequately express and am grateful to them for publishing this work of my heart.

I also appreciate various friends who read portions of this book in process and made suggestions. One who stands out in doing this is Donna Higgins Smith, who, in addition to promoting my books ceaselessly in California, read a number of drafts and offered many helpful grammatical and clarity suggestions at each step of the way.

Finally, there's my wife, Nancy. For more years than I can count, she's urged me to speak and write more from my heart and less from my head. That's been good advice and has made me a better writer and speaker. And a better man too. Thank you, Nancy.

RESOURCES FOR GOING DEEPER

Below you'll find some books and workshop sites that I think you'll find helpful as you embark on living your abundant spiritual life of beauty, truth, life, and love.

Books

A Private History of Awe by Scott Russell Sanders (North Point Press, 2006). Sanders is a writer of rare talent and grace. His works, including this one, are shot through with beauty, truth, life, and love. In particular, this book invites us to experience the often-forgotten emotion of overwhelming awe as part of our spiritual journeys and in daily life.

Beauty Will Save the World: Rediscovering the Allure and Mystery of Christianity by Brian Zahnd (Charisma House, 2012). Zahnd is a pastor (Word of Life Church), and his pastor's heart shows as he helps us look at how the church has largely removed beauty from the Gospel in exchange for theological propositions and formulas. Zahnd's premise is that "our task is not to protest the world into a certain moral conformity, but to attract the world to the saving beauty of Christ."

Bridge to Wonder: Art as a Gospel of Beauty by Cecilia González-Andrieu (Baylor University Press, 2012). Named one of *America* magazine's most promising young theologians, González-Andrieu draws both on the metaphor of the Golden Gate Bridge in relation to theology and art and from her Hispanic roots as she examines how "artists through the creation or extension of symbols witness to the existence of and participate actively in the work of mediating revelation . . . while [moving] humanity toward revelatory moments."

Culture Care: Reconnecting with Beauty for Our Common Life by Makoto Fujimura (InterVarsity Press, 2017). Fujimura, the founder of the International Arts Movement (https://internationalartsmovement .org), is one of the most articulate contemporary voices on beauty and faith. In *Culture Care*, he makes a case for cultural stewardship and for being creative in ways that feed our spirits and culture's soul as well.

Divine Beauty: The Invisible Embrace by John O'Donohue (Bantam, 2004). O'Donohue is one of the best-loved writers on Celtic spirituality, and in this book he mingles Celtic traditions with classical and medieval ones regarding the arts and nature. He invites the reader to go on a pilgrimage of seeking beauty everywhere.

Landscapes of the Sacred: Geography and Narrative in American Spirituality by Belden C. Lane (Johns Hopkins University Press, 2001). Belden Lane's writings first introduced me to the concept of paying attention in love—and how that attention changes me as I see the daily ordinary. This wonderful book is an exploration of how place—where we are—matters to our spiritual lives, through the lenses of Native American life, early French and Spanish settlers in the Americas, the Puritans in New England, and more.

The Beauty of the Infinite: The Aesthetics of Christian Truth by David Bentley Hart (Eerdmans, 2004). I first read this exploration and exposition on "theological aesthetics" after it was recommended by a wise and well-read friend of mine shortly after it came out. I was not disappointed. It's dense, but then how could a book that covers Kant, Hegel, Nietzsche, and Heidegger, while looking at a Christian understanding of beauty through four lenses (the Trinity, creation, salvation, and eschaton), not be? For those who are serious about theology and metaphysics and want to wade into deep water, this is just the book.

The Magnificent Story: Uncovering a Gospel of Beauty, Goodness, and Truth by James Bryan Smith (InterVarsity Press, 2017). James Bryan Smith has long been an advocate of the beauty in Christian faith and love (his other titles include *The Good and Beautiful God* and *The Good and Beautiful Life*). *The Magnificent Story* helps us look at the stories we tell about Christian faith and how they influence how we live out that faith for just okay lives or abundant living.

The Quiet Eye: A Way of Looking at Pictures by Sylvia Shaw Judson (Regnery, 1954). Shaw, a twentieth-century Quaker sculptor best known for her *Bird Girl* statue that was featured on the cover of *Midnight in the Garden of Good and Evil*, compiled this little book of art and meditations in 1954. It's been in print ever since. I have given many copies of it to friends around the world and keep my own, well-worn edition on the corner of my writing desk. I reach for it whenever I need a moment or two of beauty, truth, life, or love.

Workshops and Seminars

Ghost Ranch (https://www.ghostranch.org/education/find-retreat-workshop/) hosts workshops on art, music, writing, and much more in the evocative arid high desert Georgia O'Keeffe called home. Since 1955 it's been a national education and retreat center owned by the Presbyterian Church (USA).

The Fujimura Institute (https://internationalartsmovement.org/events) offers special gatherings, lectures, concerts, readings, and more. The institute's events occur in New York City (its home base), around the world, and online.

The Glen Workshop (https://imagejournal.org/glenworkshop) is a powerful week of morning workshops and afternoons and evenings featuring readings, field trips, panel conversations, concerts, open mics, worship services, all in a community of fellow seekers of beauty and faith.

CHAPTER NOTES

Chapter 1: The Ideals Life, or The Abundant Life?

7   *"I came so that they might have life and have it more abundantly."*   John 10:10 (NABRE).

7   *"The mass of men [and women] lead lives of quiet desperation."*   Henry D. Thoreau, *Walden* (New York: Thomas Y. Crowell, 1910), 8.

7   *A recent survey revealed that the United States was out-happied by Costa Rica.* "World Happiness Report," 2017, http://worldhappiness.report/ed/2017/.

8   *"love, joy, peace, forbearance, kindness, goodness, faithfulness, gentleness and self-control."*   Galatians 5:22–23 (NIV).

12   *"Jesus calls us from the worship."*   Cecil Frances Alexander, "Jesus Calls Us, O'er the Tumult" (1852, public domain).

Chapter 2: Beauty—Engaging the Divine Spark

15   *"Begin with the beautiful, and it leads you to the true."*   Bishop Robert Barron with John Allen Jr., *To Light a Fire on the Earth: Proclaiming the Gospel in a Secular Age* (New York: Image, 2017), 132.

15   *"Beauty: the quality or aggregate of qualities in a person or thing that gives pleasure to the senses or pleasurably exalts the mind or spirit."*   *Merriam-Webster Dictionary*, s.v. "beauty,"-https://www.merriam-webster.com/dictionary/beauty,

16   *"Beauty is a nectar which intoxicates the soul."*   T. C. Henley, "Beauty," *People & Howitts Journal of Literature and Art and Popular Progress* (London: Willoughby, n.d.), 353.

17   *"What is beauty in a poem? It's more than just lovely sounds, and it has to be saying something that's true."*   Ian McEwan, *The Children Act*, screenplay (2017).

20   *"My country's skies are bluer than the ocean / And sunlight beams on clover leaf and pine."*   Lloyd Stone, "This Is My Song" (Dayton, OH; Lorenz, 1934).

21   *"Perpetua shouted out with joy as the sword pierced her, for she wanted to taste some of the pain . . ."*   *Lives of Roman Christian Women*, ed. and trans. Carolinne White (London: Penguin, 2010).

22   *"as a man after God's heart."*   See Acts 13:22 (NIV).

22   *"He has made everything beautiful in its time."*   Ecclesiastes 3:11 (NIV).

25   *"to gaze on the beauty of the LORD."*   Psalm 27:4 (NIV).

26   *"Have you wept at anything during the past year?"*   Frederick Buechner, *Listening to Your Life: Daily Meditations with Frederick Buechner*, ed. George Connor (New York: HarperCollins, 1992), 7.

27 *"Beauty will save the world."*   Fyodor Dostoevsky, *The Idiot*, trans. Alan Meyers (Oxford: Oxford University Press, 2008), 555.

27 *"Our primal source was beauty, and we pant for it ever and again."*   Martin Farquhar Tupper, "Of Beauty," in *Proverbial Philosophy* (Boston: Phillips, Samson, 1851), 165.

27 *"It is in our bodies that redemption takes place. . . . I learn through my hands and my eyes and my skin what I could never learn through my brain."*   M. C. Richards, *Centering: In Pottery, Poetry and the Person* (Middletown, CT: Wesleyan University Press, 1989), 15.

30 *"Frost on the window never the same."*   Jim Croegaert, "Why Do We Hunger For Beauty?" (Meadowgreen Music Co./Heart of the Matter Music, 1989).

30 *"Try walking around with a child who's going, 'Wow, wow!'"*   Anne Lamott, *Bird by Bird: Some Instructions on Writing and Life* (New York: Anchor, 1995), 110.

31 *"Every child has known God, / Not the God of names"*   Hafiz, *The Gift: Poems by the Great Sufi Master*, trans. Daniel Ladinsky (New York: Penguin Putnam, 1999), 270.

32 *"Let all creation help you to praise God."*   *Flowers of the Passion: Thoughts of Saint Paul of the Cross*, trans. Ella A. Mulligan (New York: Benziger Brothers, 1893), 88.

32 *"Whenever beauty overwhelms us, whenever wonder silences our chattering hopes and worries, we are close to worship."*   Richard C Cabot, *What Men Live By* (New York: Houghton Mifflin, 1914), 270.

32 *"In my old Catholic neighborhood in Chicago."*   Marianne Borouch, "Worlds Old and New," in *Falling Toward Grace: Images of Religion and Culture from the Heartland*, ed J. Kent Calder and Susan Neville (Indianapolis: The Polis Center and Indiana University Press, 1998), 99–100.

34 *"In the beginning God created the heavens and the earth."*   Genesis 1:1 (NIV).

35 *"Creation, we are taught, is not an act that happened once upon a time, once and for ever."*   Abraham J. Heschel, *Between God and Man: An Interpretation of Judaism*, ed. Fritz A Rothschild (New York: Simon & Schuster, 1959), 229.

36 *"Let the beauty we love be what we do."*   Coleman Barks, *Rumi: The Book of Love: Poems of Ecstasy and Longing* (San Francisco: HarperSanFrancisco, 2003), 123.

37 *"If a thing is ugly, I think we need to ask questions about it. How did it get that way? What else is wrong?"*   "On the Natural Order of Things: An Interview with Wendell Berry by Lauren Wilcox," posted by Austin

Bailey, "Wendell Berry Puts Us All on Blast," Heifer International, October 2, 2018, https://www.heifer.org/join-the-conversation/blog/2018/October/wendell-berry-puts-us-all-on-blast.html.

40 *"the truth is, until we have taken the time to discover and affirm who we really are."* Laurence Boldt, *How to Find the Work You Love* (New York: Penguin Compass, 2004).

40 *"We see the beauty within and cannot say no."* Dave Eggers, *A Heartbreaking Work of Staggering Genius: A Memoir Based on a True Story* (New York: Simon and Schuster, 2001), 7.

41 *"a striking resemblance to Jesus that people sense they have encountered him when they encounter us."* Gordon Crosby, "Becoming the Authentic Church," Beloved Community, April 29, 2006, http://www.belovedcommunity .info/faith/faithfulmoderates/becomingauthenticchurch.htm.

Chapter 3: Truth—Living in Utter Rightness

43 *"If our true nature is permitted to guide our life, we grow healthy, fruitful and happy."* Abraham Maslow, quoted by Laurence Boldt, *How to Find the Work You Love* (New York: Penguin Compass, 2004).

43 *"Truth carries life-giving properties for the soul."* Hal M. Helms, *Echoes of Eternity* (Brewster, MA: Paraclete Press, 1996), 225.

46 *"I will make justice the measuring line / and righteousness the plumb line."* Isaiah 28:17 (NIV).

46 *"This is what he showed me."* Amos 7:7–8 (NIV).

47 *"the philosophical study of the structures of experience and consciousness."* "Phenomenology (Philosophy)," Wikipedia, accessed July 31, 2019 https://en.wikipedia.org/wiki/Phenomenology_(philosophy).

47 *"If there is something more excellent than the truth, then that is God; if not, then truth itself is God."* Wayne P. Pomerleau, *Twelve Great Philosophers: A Historical Introduction to Human Nature* (New York: Ardsley House, 1997), 77.

47 *"a rectitude perceptible by the mind alone."* David S. Hogg, *Anselm of Canterbury: The Beauty of Theology* (New York: Routledge, 2004), 138.

47 *"Truth resides, in its primary aspect, in the intellect."* Thomas Aquinas, *Summa theologica*, Volume 1 (New York: Benziger Brothers, 1947), 93.

49 *"While being interviewed on Meet the Press Giuliani famously said, 'Truth isn't truth.'"* Caroline Kenny, "Rudy Giuliani Says 'Truth Isn't Truth'" *CNN Politics*, August 19, 2018, https://www.cnn.com/2018/08/19/politics/rudy -giuliani-truth-isnt-truth/index.html.

49 *"Truthiness is 'What I say is right, and [nothing] anyone else says could possibly be true.'"* Stephen Colbert, *The Colbert Report*, October 17, 2005, http://www .cc.com/video-clips/63ite2/the-colbert-report-the-word---truthiness.

49 *"Show me your ways, LORD."* Psalm 25:4 (NIV).

49 *"then you will know the truth, and the truth will set you free."* John 8:32 (NIV).

50 *"I would be true, for there are those who trust me"* H. A. Walter, "I Would Be True" (public domain), https://hymnary.org/text/i_would_be_true_for_ there_are_those.

50 *"We cannot know the whole truth, which belongs to God alone."* Wendell Berry, *It All Turns on Affection: The Jefferson Lecture and Other Essays* (Berkeley: Counterpoint, 2012), 27.

51 *"I saw it was the truth, and I could not deny it."* Margaret Askew Fell Fox, *The Life of Margaret Fox, Wife of George Fox, Comp. from Her Own Narrative* (Philadelphia: Association for of Friends for the Diffusion of Religious and Useful Knowledge, 1859), 8.

52 *"About a dozen years ago I became critically ill and I have a vivid memory of looking down on myself on the bed."* Jennifer Faulkner, "Out of the Depths," *The Friend* 140 (1982): 805–6.

53 *"Therefore everyone who hears these words of mine and puts them into practice is like a wise man who built his house on the rock."* Matthew 7:24 (NIV).

54 *"If you are what you should be, you will set the whole world ablaze!"* Mary Rice Hasson, ed., *Promise and Challenge, Catholic Women Reflect on Feminism, Complementarity, and the Church* (Huntington, IN: Our Sunday Visitor, 2015), 104.

56 *"true self is the self with which we arrive on earth, the self that simply wants us to be who we were born to be."* Parker Palmer, *On The Brink of Everything: Grace, Gravity, and Getting Old* (Williston, VT: Berrett-Koehler, 2018), 75.

56 *"For a stone is called true, which possesses the nature proper to a stone."* Thomas Aquinas, *Summa theologica*, Volume 1 (New York: Benziger Brothers, 1947), 90.

56 *" 'I tell you,' he replied, 'if they keep quiet, the stones will cry out'."* Luke 19:40 (NIV).

57 *"Some days, /Like this one / I have to stay away."* Catharine Phillips, "Voice," *All Will Be Well. Period.* (blog), April 12, 2012, https://allwillbewellperiod. blogspot.com/2012/04/voice.html.

58 *"I wish I might emphasize how a life becomes simplified when dominated by faithfulness to a few concerns."* Thomas R Kelly, *A Testament of Devotion* (New York: Harper & Row, 1941), 110.

61   *"The integrity of the upright guides them."* Proverbs 11:3 (NIV).

62   *"Before I can tell my life what I want to do with it, I must listen to my life telling me who I am."* Beth Booram, *Starting Something New: Spiritual Direction for Your God-Given Dream* (Downers Gove, IL: InterVarsity Press, 2015), 41.

66   *"I prefer to be true to myself, even at the hazard of incurring the ridicule of others, rather than to be false, and to incur my own abhorrence."* Frederick Douglass, *Narrative of the Life of Frederick Douglass: An American Slave* (New York; Cosimo Classics, 2008), 19.

71   *"The truth is never far from your heart and your spirit."* Wayne Muller, *How, Then, Shall We Live?* (New York: Bantam, 1996), 93.

Chapter 4: Life—Vim, Vigor, and Vivacity

73   *"You make known to me the path of life"* Psalm 16:11 (NIV).

73   *"Life is the art of drawing without an eraser."* John W. Gardner, quoted in Joseph Demakis, ed., *The Ultimate Book of Quotations* (Raleigh, NC: Lulu, 2012), 104.

76   *"robust energy and enthusiasm."* *Merriam-Webster Dictionary*, s.v."vim", https://www.merriam-webster.com/dictionary/vim.

80   *"Here is the unfailing attraction of the life in Christ. It is a life which even to old age, is always on the upgrade."* William Littleboy, *Swarthmore Lecture: The Day of Our Visitation* (London: Headly Brothers, 1917), 55.

83   *"I am the way and the truth and the life."* John 14:6 (NIV).

83   *"I came so that they might have life and have it more abundantly."* John 10:10 (NABRE).

86   *"The central issue is always, 'Where is the Spirit leading you?'"* Patricia Loring, quoted by J. Brent Bill, *Sacred Compass: The Way of Spiritual Discernment* (Brewster, MA: Paraclete Press, 2008), 59.

91   *"there's no there there."* Gertrude Stein, *Everybody's Autobiography* (New York: Vintage, 1973).

91   *"To feed my soul with beauty till I die; / To give my hands a pleasant task to do; / To keep my heart forever filled anew / With dreams and wonders which the days supply."* William Stanley Braithwaite, "This Is My Life," in *The House of Falling Leaves With Other Poems* (Boston: John W. Luce, 1908), 101.

92   *"The most precious things of life are near at hand, without money and without price."* John Burroughs, *John Burroughs' America: Selections from the Writings of the Naturalist* (Mineola, NY: Dover, 1997), xiv, 3.

94   *"But I gave joy to my mother / I made my lover smile."* Iris Dement, "My Life" (Iowa City, IA: Songs of Iris, 1993).

95   *"Oh, the good life, full of fun, seems to be the ideal."*   Jack Reardon and Sacha Distel, "The Good Life" (Los Angeles: Warner/Chappell Music, 1962).

Chapter 5: Love—Being Directed by Heart

97   *"The greatest of these is love."*   1 Corinthians 13:13 (NIV).

97   *"The whole worth of a kind deed lies in the love that inspires it."*   The Talmud, Sukkah 49b, quoted in Lois Tverberg, *Walking in the Dust of Rabbi Jesus: How the Jewish Words of Jesus Can Change Your Life* (Grand Rapids: Zondervan, 2013), 133.

98   *"We're all still beginners."*   Linford Detweiler, "All My Favorite People" (Vancouver, BC: Scampering Songs Publishing; Brentwood, TN: Ariose Music Group, 2010).

98   *"I will show you the most excellent way."*   1 Corinthians 12:31 (NIV).

99   *"Firstborn of Mary, provocative preacher, itinerant teacher, outsider's choice."*   John Bell, "First Born of Mary" (Glasgow: Wild Goose Resource Group, 1998).

99   *"I love mankind—it's people I can't stand."*   Robert L. Short, *The Gospel According to Peanuts* (New York: Bantam, 1968), 107.

99   *"the infinite love of God."*   George Fox, *Journal*, ed. John L. Nickalls (London: Religious Society of Friends, 1975), 19.

100   *"Every day, / I walk by your house and bring you flowers."*   Christine Kelly, "Unrequited Lover," *Friends Journal*, March 1998, 19.

106   *"Once a person learns to read the signs of love and thus to believe it, love leads him into the open field wherein he himself can love."*   Hans Urs von Balthasar, *Love Alone Is Credible*, trans. David C. Schindler (San Francisco: Ignatius, 2004).

106   *"the hands to help others. It has the feet to hasten to the poor and needy."*   William C. Graham, *100 Days Closer to Christ* (Collegeville, MN: Liturgical Press, 2014), 92.

107   *"For one human being to love another human being: that is perhaps the most difficult task that has been entrusted to us."*   Rainier Maria Rilke, *Letters to a Young Poet*, trans. M. D. Herter Norton (New York: W. W. Norton, 1934), 42.

107   *"Love your neighbor as yourself."*   Matthew 22:39 (NIV).

108   *"Love is the hardest lesson in Christianity; but, for that reason, it should be most our care to learn it."*   William Penn, "Maxim 548," in *A Collection of the Works of William Penn in Two Volumes* (London: J. Sowle, 1726), 843.

109   *"To live with the Spirit of God is to be a listener"* and *"To live with the Spirit of God is to be a lover."*   Jessica Powers, "To Live with the Spirit," in *The Selected Poetry of Jessica Powers*, ed. Regina Siegfried and Robert Morneau (Washington,

DC: ICS, 1999), 38.

111 *"Love your enemies, do good to them, and lend to them without expecting to get anything back."*   Luke 6:35 (NIV).

111 *"All you need is love."*   John Lennon and Paul McCartney, "All You Need Is Love" (Nashville: Sony/ATV Music Publishing LLC, 1967).

112 *"Love gave me the key to my vocation."*   Hans Urs von Balthasar, *Two Sisters in the Spirit: Thérèse of Lisieux and Elizabeth of the Trinity*, trans. Donald Nichols, Anne Englund Nash, and Dennis Martin (San Francisco: Ignatius, 2004), 198.

113 *"What is love? What shall I say of it, or how shall I in words express its nature?"*   *The Works of Isaac Penington* (Sherwood, NY: David Heston, 1862), 2:376.

113 *joy, peace, forbearance, kindness, goodness, faithfulness, gentleness and self-control.*   Galatians 5:22–23 (NIV).

113 *"love was the first motion."*   John Woolman, *The Journal and Major Essays of John Woolman*, ed. Phillips P. Moulton (New York: Oxford University Press, 1971), 127.

114 *"to spend some time with the Indians."*   Woolman, *Journal*, 127.

119 *"flies, runs, leaps for joy."*   Thomas à Kempis, *The Inner Life*, trans. Leo Sherley-Price (New York: Penguin, 1952), 16.

Chapter 6: Weaving Beauty, Truth, Life, and Love into the Tapestry of Life

121 *"Love is the fruit of beauty."*   Satish Kumar, interview in *Heron Dance*, issue 23.

123 *"We know that in all things God works for the good of those who love him."*   Romans 8:28 (NIV).

124 *"The time of fear is over. The time of hope has begun."*   Tristan Bernard, quoted in C. Peter Fleck, *Come as You Are: Reflections on the Revelations of Everyday Life* (Boston: Beacon, 1993), 46.

125 *"For now we see only a reflection as in a mirror; then we shall see face to face. Now I know in part; then I shall know fully, even as I am fully known."*   1 Corinthians 13:12 (NIV).

PERMISSIONS

ABOUT BRENT

In addition to his ministry of writing, Brent also enjoys a ministry of leading workshops and speaking. Some of his most popular workshops are the following:

- Life Lessons from A Bad Quaker is a light-hearted, but serious, workshop for anyone who is bad at being good. With whimsy, humor, and wisdom, workshop participants will explore how to live a life that is simple yet satisfying, peaceful yet strong.
- The Sacred Compass: Spiritual Practices for Discernment is a workshop for those who want to learn discernment as a life process.
- Writing from the Heart: Telling Your Soul's Stories is for those who want to unlock their spiritual stories.
- Seeking and Finding God in the Verbs (with Jennie Isbell) is a workshop that guides participants in crafting fresh, authentic prayers.
- Awaken Your Senses (with Beth Booram) is geared toward helping people experience God in new ways by using their bodies and souls.
- Being Quiet: The Practice of Holy Silence is based on Quaker silence and teaches how to be quiet and still in our souls amid the clamor of everyday life.

If you would like more information about Brent's writing his spirituality workshops and retreats, or if you would like to contact him about other speaking engagements, you can reach him through his website at www.brentbill.com or via e-mail at brentbil@brentbill.com.

ABOUT PARACLETE PRESS

WHO WE ARE

As the publishing arm of the Community of Jesus, Paraclete Press presents a full expression of Christian belief and practice—from Catholic to Evangelical, from Protestant to Orthodox, reflecting the ecumenical charism of the Community and its dedication to sacred music, the fine arts, and the written word. We publish books, recordings, sheet music, and video/DVDs that nourish the vibrant life of the church and its people.

WHAT WE ARE DOING

Books

PARACLETE PRESS BOOKS show the richness and depth of what it means to be Christian. While Benedictine spirituality is at the heart of who we are and all that we do, our books reflect the Christian experience across many cultures, time periods, and houses of worship.

We have many series, including *Paraclete Essentials; Paraclete Fiction; Paraclete Poetry; Paraclete Giants;* and for children and adults, *All God's Creatures,* books about animals and faith; and *San Damiano Books,* focusing on Franciscan spirituality. Others include *Voices from the Monastery* (men and women monastics writing about living a spiritual life today), *Active Prayer,* and new for young readers: *The Pope's Cat.* We also specialize in gift books for children on the occasions of Baptism and First Communion, as well as other important times in a child's life, and books that bring creativity and liveliness to any adult spiritual life.

The Mount Tabor Books series focuses on the arts and literature as well as liturgical worship and spirituality; it was created in conjunction with the Mount Tabor Ecumenical Centre for Art and Spirituality in Barga, Italy.

Music

THE PARACLETE RECORDINGS label represents the internationally acclaimed choir *Gloriæ Dei Cantores,* the *Gloriæ Dei Cantores Schola,* and the other instrumental artists of the *Arts Empowering Life Foundation.*

Paraclete Press is the exclusive North American distributor for the Gregorian chant recordings from St. Peter's Abbey in Solesmes, France. Paraclete also carries all of the Solesmes chant publications for Mass and the Divine Office, as well as their academic research publications.

In addition, PARACLETE PRESS SHEET MUSIC publishes the work of today's finest composers of sacred choral music, annually reviewing over 1,000 works and releasing between 40 and 60 works for both choir and organ.

Video

Our video/DVDs offer spiritual help, healing, and biblical guidance for a broad range of life issues including grief and loss, marriage, forgiveness, facing death, understanding suicide, bullying, addictions, Alzheimer's, and Christian formation.

Learn more about us at our website:
www.paracletepress.com,
or call us toll-free at 1-800-451-5006.

SCAN
TO
READ
MORE

YOU MAY ALSO BE INTERESTED IN

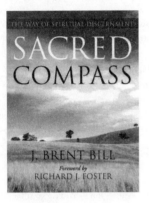